D1572333

1849
The Oldest Store
In Contimous Operation
I Know Of
Moses

U. S. POST-OFFICE
1850 LUCKENBACH, TX. 197
Velvet
America's
Smoothest
ROBBYN DODD

LUCKENBACH TEXAS

The CENTER of the UNIVERSE

THE STORY

BECKY CROUCH PATTERSON

FOREWORD BY
JOHN PHILLIP SANTOS

LUCKENBACH TEXAS
Center of the Universe
The Story

Inquiries and order requests should be addressed to
Becky Patterson Books
www.beckycrouchpatterson.com

SECOND EDITION, 2022

ISBN 978-0-692-12728-5

Cataloging-in-publication data

1. German Texans—Texas Hill Country social life and customs
2. Hondo Crouch—folklore 3. Texas "Outlaw" music—memoir

Cover design by Shauna Dodds
Cover photo of author by D. Foster
Foreword by John Phillip Santos

Printed in the United States of America
at OneTouchPoint-Southwest in Austin, Texas

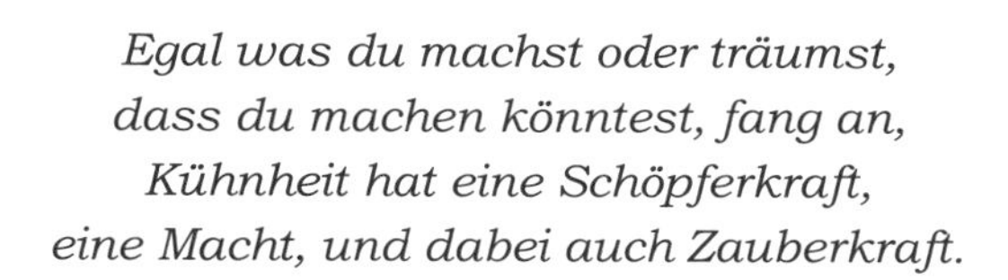

Egal was du machst oder träumst,
dass du machen könntest, fang an,
Kühnheit hat eine Schöpferkraft,
eine Macht, und dabei auch Zauberkraft.

Whatever you do, or dream you can do, begin.
Boldness has a genius, power, and magic to it.

– Johann Wolfgang von Goethe

Blessed are the gypsies, the makers of music,
the artists, writers, dreamers of dreams,
wanderers and vagabonds; children of misfits:
For they teach us to see the world through beautiful eyes.

– Unknown

"It'll never happen again.
That was a time and place."

– Jessi Colter

RICHARD PRUITT

To

HONDO

The Sunday Mayor

of Luckenbach

Real. Imagined. Remembered.

TABLE of CONTENTS

FOREWORDS 11
PROLOGUE: The "Queen Mother of Nashville" Calls 15
WHO WAS HONDO CROUCH? 19
A Genuine Texas Tall Tale 19
To Tell the Truth 25
"WHERE in the HELL is LUCKENBACH?" 27
"IS LUCKENBACH A REAL TOWN?" 31
"Let's Buy a Town" 33
The Luckenbach Regulars 38
Porfie Cantu—Number One Regular 40
Juan and Ken: The Luckenbach Air Force 42
Zip Zimmerman—Outlaw Security 45
THE IMAGINEER (authorized distributor) 49
The Ladies-Only Chili Bust 53
Cedar Creek Clippings—Chili Wars 57
Terlingua 59
The Luckenbach Great World's Fair 65
The Return of the Mud Daubers to Luckenbach 72
The Non-Buy Centennial 1976 75
¡VIVA TERLINGUA! 1973 80
Scamp Walker Meets Scamp Hondo 80
Birth of Outlaw Music 86
Luckenbach Plugged In 87
You Don't Know What You Got Til You Got Nunn 93
"I'M NOT HERE ANYMORE" 99
Last Sightings of Hondo 99
Jerry Jeff Sightings 108
"A Man Must Carry On" 111
"LET'S GO to LUCKENBACH, TEXAS—BACK to the BASICS" 113
Guy Clark 116
Waylon Jennings 119
BACK to the BASICS 122
Hondo's Truck 122
Standing Ovation for the Luckenbach Dance Hall 126
Miranda Lambert Gets Back to the Basics at Luckenbach 134
¡VIVA LUCKENBACH! 1993 138
The Parade 145

WILLIE'S COMIN'! 149
The Great Domino Confrontation 149
The Fourth of July Picnics 152
Pic-Nix 159
THE LUCKENBACH MONTHLY MOON CHRONICLES 177
On the Road Again 178
Luckenbach Royalty Mr. and Mrs. Pat Green 178
Steve and Harley, Luckenbach's Short-Lived Radio Show 180
How Much Food Could a Chuckwagon Chuck If a Chuckwagon Could Chuck Food? (All 'n Nall) 182
Virgil Holdman: Our One-Man Band 187
Abbey Road's Road to Luckenbach 189
The Lost Children of Luckenbach (today known as old-timers) 190
Jimmy Lee Jones: Luckenbach's Weekday Bartender/Fire Marshal/ Chicken Farmer/Singer 193
Letters to the Moon 196
Editorial from Editor Maggie Montgomery 198
The Big Littlehorn Battle 199
THE HILL COUNTRY TRAIL OF FAME 201
The Treaty—Baron von Meusebach, Peacemaker 202
"The Freethinkers" and The Civil War 207
"The Hangebund," or "Hanging Gang" 209
Battle of the Nueces 211
The "Luckenbach Bushwhackers" 213
Sophisticated Sisterdale 215
JACOB BRODBECK—Luckenbach's Inventor, Educator, Musician 217
FESTS 225
Grapetown and Luckenbach: Singing and Shooting Fests 226
The Dast Ist Alles Fest (That's All) 231
WILL THE CIRCLE BE UNBROKEN 233
Remembering Sheriff Marge and Ethel the Guinea Hen, and the Healing Power of Music 233
We Were Counted 241
The Original Magic of Luckenbach, Texas (The First of the Pickers' Circles) 246
EPILOGUE: Hondo Crouch, Reinventor 251
ABOUT THE AUTHOR 259
BIBLIOGRAPHY 260
IN APPRECIATION 265

ROBBYN DODD

HONDO'S EAGLE WATCHES OVER ALL IN BAR
–LUCKENBACH TEXAS

FOREWORDS

Becky Crouch Patterson, a true literary alchemist, has taken a tall tale and revealed within it a hidden saga of how her family, particularly her dad, Hondo Crouch, a sui generis Texas Classic, tale-spinner extraordinaire, Hill Country trickster mystic, legendary mayor of Luckenbach, came to embody, manifest, and celebrate a new way of being Texan that literally changed the world. For readers who have followed the unfolding tale begun in her first two family chronicles,*Hondo* (*My Father*), 1979, and *The Ranch That Was Us*, 2012, we have come to know how Becky's family emerged out of the rich history of 19th century German immigrants to the Texas Hill Country—perhaps unsurprisingly, from ancestors who had been a part of the Freethinker's movement that was the target of a shocking and notorious 1862 massacre of Freethinkers on the Nueces River at the hands of a band of Texas Confederate Cavalrymen.

Becky's tersely lyrical writing about her family, about her father, shows that free thought was not extinguished, and that her family, the Crouches and the Stielers, had an appointment with the destiny of Texas itself. This book completes that saga, telling us how Hondo, by force of imagination and irrepressible mirth, took the Podunk, broke-down, has-been crook in the road that Luckenbach was and turned it into the Mecca of a new Texan freedom of thought and creativity, nurturing the early work of such legends as Willie, Waylon and the boys, like Jerry Jeff Walker, Gary P. Nunn, Ray Wylie Hubbard, Guy Clark, Townes Van Zandt, to mention a few of the "outlaw" poets who loved to come to Luckenbach. Out of that oak grove setting on South Grape Creek, Hondo somehow managed to rock the world.

They lived Texan identity as an ethic of radical liberty and borderless pranks, embracing a redemptive freedom where anything could happen, and it did.

You thumb tack your jerky to the dorm room ceiling. You use a skunk's skull as a lamplight. You carve and whittle spoons. You play your guitar and sing cowboy songs or Mexican corridos.

As Hondo once wrote in a kind of manifesto under his *nombre de mascarada*, Peter Cedarstacker:

> *"Luckenbach is a state of mind.*
> *Luckenbach is a free state."*

As much of a one-of-a-kind icon as Hondo was, he was also the legatee of the classical myth lineages of Texas, one that he got directly from his upbringing in uniquely rustic Hondo, Texas, and from his early tutelage with this myth's living master, J. Frank Dobie—Hondo's teacher during his first year at the University of Texas.

In truth, Hondo lived Dobie's dream, and Luckenbach was Hondo's Brigadoon.

I witnessed the world that Hondo created, though we never met personally. As a high schooler visiting Luckenbach on a Saturday, I watched him quietly preside over circles of singers and songwriters, occasionally offering some uncanny intervention or tale.

"On Thursdays our army practices. We practice losin' so we can get foreign aid."

There was an audacity about their lyrical freedom, their home-grown artistic passion, a spark that helped to ignite me and my own search for the stories and meanings of Texas.

I had invited Hondo to come to tell his tales at a literary festival at the University of Notre Dame in 1976, only to be saddened when he suddenly took his leave from this world. That festival was dedicated to the memory of Hondo Crouch, Imagineer. The world awaits the wider discovery of Hondo and his Luckenbach vision. He never glorified what he so nimbly and grandly achieved there.

As he put it, "I wanted Luckenbach for the same reason a dog buries a bone. So no other dog'll get it."

Becky's deeply moving testimonio, now spanning three tomes(!), guarantees that Hondo and Luckenbach will never be forgotten, and that the world has its ample and long-overdue chance to meet him, too.

– *John Phillip Santos*

Manhattitlán,
May 17, 2018

The story of Luckenbach, Texas is long overdue. Becky Crouch Patterson has finally given us the definitive one, filling in the blanks of the history and goings-ons, the pranks, and the 'play-likes' (pronounced 'p'likes') of Luckenbach since Hondo Crouch decided he wanted to 'buy his own town'! It was the perfect stage for Hondo to perform his magic, and magic occurs on a daily basis still. And believe me; magic takes you to a whole other universe. Ms. Patterson obviously inherited her father's playfulness and storytelling ability that she so skillfully shares with us here. It's time we started looking back to Luckenbach, so here it is! Enjoy!

– Gary P. Nunn
Feb. 27, 2018

Becky Crouch, Hondo's daughter, had a bird's eye view of all things Luckenbach. If there's anybody who knows how it all went down, has a pile of told and untold stories, it's this gal.

– Bob Livingston

ROBBYN DODD

PROLOGUE
The "Queen Mother of Nashville" Calls

In 1979, the year my book *Hondo, My Father* came out, my phone rang at my home in San Antonio, Texas. "Becky, this is Mae Axton," the voice on the other end of the line started off. "Our mutual friend Rex Allen, Jr. gave me your book. It's fabulous! Listen to this," she exclaimed as she read parts she'd underlined. "And listen to this!" She read more. "I believe in this book so much I want you to come to Nashville and I'll promote it for free!"

"Who is Mae Axton?" I asked my husband Dow after I hung up.

"She's the mother of Hoyt. He wrote 'Greenback Dollar' and 'Joy to the World.' Mae co-wrote 'Heartbreak Hotel' for Elvis and invented his favorite peanut butter and banana sandwich."

Mae Axton, I learned, was the best publicist to the country stars anyone could have. She was also one of Nashville's most industrious persons. More importantly, she put her words into action. So, to have her call little ol' me was something.

For a week, we stayed in her palatial colonial-style house in Hendersonville, outside of Nashville, while she promoted and entertained us, spending her time and her own money on us. My three sons Ren, Kit, and Sky 11, 8 and 2, respectively, came along. Kit will never forget staying in Hoyt's bedroom and seeing the big green stuffed frog in a chair wearing a T-shirt that said "Jeremiah." I'll never forget that Sky peed in Hoyt's big four-poster bed. Dow will never forget the sole contents in Mae's icebox: six-oz. green-bottled Coca-Colas and a quart of cream for her coffee.

Mae took us to radio stations, and even wrangled a guest appearance for us on Ralph Emory's TV show where he asked Dow to sing not one but two songs. Backstage at the Grand Ole Opry, Tex Ritter's wife gave the boys Goo-Goo bars. Roy Acuff came up behind 11-year-old Ren, put his arms around his chest, and pulled him up to his own chest.

I was charmed by Minnie Pearl, born Sarah Ophelia Colley. To me, she and my father Hondo Crouch both appeared like country bumpkins, she in her hat with dangling price tag and Hondo always in faded denim and broken hat. Both were actually very sophisticated, educated and genteel. Hondo was as talented as the star entertainers, yet totally uncommercial and unambitious. His stage was any street corner or oat field. He and Millie Pearl would have gotten along just fine.

Mae sent a TV camera along with us to the Governor's Mansion where we had lunch with "Honey" Alexander, wife of Governor Lamar Alexander. I knew her as Leslie Buhler from Victoria, Texas, when she was my roommate at St. Stephen's Episcopal High School in Austin. As we approached the mansion there were several Big Wheel trikes and bikes scattered all over the manicured formal grounds. When I presented Honey with my book she exclaimed, "I already have one, Becky!"

The one thing Mae asked me on the phone that first day was "Why didn't you call your book Luckenbach?" In the music world a song about Luckenbach, Texas had skyrocketed to become the nation's Number One cross-over country song faster than any other, courtesy of Waylon Jennings and Willie Nelson. "Everyone's heard about Luckenbach," she said, meaning the song. "No one knows who Hondo Crouch is!"

Such was Mae Axton's hospitable, gracious gesture to try to launch Hondo out of Texas. It wouldn't take much longer.

The "Luckenbach" I write about here centers around the short-lived years my father, Hondo Crouch, had it, 1970–1976. There were the Before Hondo years and the After Hondo years. But the Hondo years were the years of great imagination, magic, and music.

After Hondo passed away in 1976, "That Song," which launched it into national fame, for better or worse, almost wiped the fragile place off the map. The public it brought swarming to the tiny town had to be dealt with. Retailers stamped "Luckenbach" on everything from cans of chili, to T-shirts, beer, and golf balls. Luckenbach is a permanent landmark now. And, for better or worse, it's become an iconic Texas brand, like the Dallas Cowboys or Lone Star Beer.

I have watched people come and go over the past 44 years, people who have searched out, found and enjoyed Luckenbach, many of them trying to recapture that original feeling of significant insignificance.

What started out as being a 167-year-old stage for Hondo, a regional character, humorist, raconteur, and state folk hero, would turn into a universal place—the center of the universe—just because it stayed simple and genuine in the hearts, eyes and minds of countless admirers.

Throughout it all, the three questions I most heard were: "Who is Hondo Crouch?"; "Is Luckenbach a real town?"; And, "Where the hell is Luckenbach?"

This book is the answer to those questions.

WHO *was* HONDO CROUCH?
A Genuine Texas Tall Tale

My father put two Texas towns on the map: Hondo and Luckenbach. John Russell "Hondo" Crouch was born in 1916 out where the West begins, in Hondo, the son of a telegraph operator for the Southern Pacific Railroad. His mom, Ione, took in borders and managed the Armstrong Hotel which they owned, where 6-year-old little Johnny danced the Charleston for tips. He went on to marry Helen Ruth "Shatzie" Stieler, daughter of Adolf Stieler, who in 1941 ruled as the "Angora Goat King of the World."

Hondo graduated from the University of Texas with degrees in Physical Education and Journalism. He got his nickname from sportswriters at U.T., where he swam in the '30s and '40s. "Who is that Hondo guy?" they asked, amazed that the desert town of Hondo, about 40 miles west of San Antonio, could produce an All-American swimmer. Already a tall-tale teller at 18, he explained, "It rained one time and I learned to swim in a cow track." He was president of the University of Texas Longhorn Hall of Honor, and in 1975 was influential in persuading the University to build the Texas Swim Center. His swimming prowess ended up landing him in the Texas Swimming Hall of Fame in 2014.

Father of four kids, Hondo grew up to be a full-time rancher, raising cattle, sheep, and Angora goats. He was a part-time swim coach at summer camps he helped start, and owned.

Hondo was also a newspaper columnist, under the pen name "Peter Cedarstacker." From 1963 to 1975 he wrote about 600 "Cedar Creek Clippings" dispatches from the mythical town of Cedar Creek for the social page of *The Comfort News*, in Comfort, Texas. He satirized politics, government, social life, racial differences, and everyday problems and celebrations.

My father's name became a household word to many Texans. *Texas Monthly* dubbed him "Most Professional Texan," and a "symbol of the state." We kids called him "Hondo" from the beginning. To us, he was like an Indian guide, reading the ground for trapping, hunting, making arrowheads, a Peter Pan-like figure whom kids loved to follow.

Hondo called himself the Mayor of Luckenbach, and his business card read "Imagineer." He was a poet, and the inspiration for the aforementioned hit song "Let's Go to Luckenbach, Texas (Back to the Basics of Love)."

He died of a heart attack on September 27, 1976, at almost 60 years of age, in Blanco, Texas. Newspaper headlines crowned him "Clown Prince of Luckenbach." Nashville lowered their flags on Music Row.

Before he died, he left an imprint on Texas folk culture as a major instigator of Texana-flavored celebrations of the '70s—zany happenings from all-female chili cook-offs to Great World's Fairs—events so popular that they almost trampled the tiny town to death. Hondo, a one-man "mirthquake," put the tiny Tex-German village of Luckenbach, the backwoods "Camelot" and "Mud Dauber Capital of the World" on the Texas map simply by being himself. With his white hair and beard, battered cowboy hat, faded jeans stuffed into his boots and a red bandana loosely circling his neck, Hondo

MONK VANCE

BECKY, 18, AND HONDO ON THEIR SHEEP AND GOAT RANCH.

philosophized, whittled, told stories, and sang Mexican *canciónes* and cowboy songs. He'd accompany himself on his guitar, which was always somewhere within reach.

With that, and not much more than an elfin smile and a mischievous twinkle in his eye, his magical personality attracted thousands to the tiny hamlet that he and a buddy had purchased on a whim. Visitors found Luckenbach not by accident, but purposely to meet the man they'd heard about.

Hondo's gift was seeing into the comedy as well as the tragedy of the human heart. His style ranged from lighthearted teasing to barbed satire, from pratfalls to rueful reflection.

The most outrageous prank he ever pulled was in 1964, on an airplane chartered for the National Folk Festival at the Smithsonian in Washington D.C. He represented Texas as a storyteller. Hondo tells it best:

> *I was walkin' out of the house to go to San Antonio to catch an airplane to Washington. I hadn't been on many airplanes before that. I saw two rattlesnake hides as I was walkin' out the door. They'd been tacked on two boards. I was stretchin' and dryin' 'em. So, I just stuffed 'em in a sack I'd slung over my back. Had that and a guitar under one arm. The rattles and about five inches of the hide stuck outta the sack and I didn't bump into* anybody *in that airport. I just rattled my rattles which were hangin' over my shoulder in front of my face.*
>
> *By the time I got on the airplane, everyone knew I had live rattlesnakes in my sack. Everyone but about eight people on the plane was going to the Folk Festival. There were mariachis, tortilla patters, cowboys in uniform, Indians in costume, Czech dancers, Cajuns from East Texas. So, I got to thinkin' that if I looked around on the floor that someone would say "What are you lookin' for?"*
>
> *There was this poor little lady that asked that wasn't with our crazy group. So, I got down on my hands and knees and started goin' down the aisle. I'll never forget her. "What are you looking for, sir?" "I lost my rattlesnakes," I replied. She went "AHHHHH!"(Hondo shot his hands up in the air, fingers spread wide apart.) Now, these are her* feet, *up in the air, not my hands!*
>
> *It went right through the airplane like a wave of hysteria. They all ran to the back. One guy said, "I'm getting outta here!" I said, "Watch that first step, it's a devil!" Then the captain came back, 'cause we'd gained about two thousand feet with all that weight rushin' to the back of the airplane.*

So, we got straightened out and landed at Dulles, in Washington. By that time, I was standin' in a crowd at the airport with the yellow roses of Texas in my arms havin' my picture taken while they were stompin' on people's handbags lookin' for those snakes. Fortunately, they arrested the wrong person.

Well, it became about as funny as sayin' 'Let's go to Cuba!' You remember when they were hijackin' all those planes? It wasn't funny at all, for about ten minutes. Nobody ever knew I pulled a trick on 'em.

And Hondo got away with that.

Then there was the time television actor Ken Curtis, who played "Festus" on the TV Western hit show *Gunsmoke*, stopped by Hondo's ranch to meet Hondo during a television filming in the surrounding Hill Country. The two men met and, so the story goes, Curtis said, "You must be Hondo." To which Hondo replied, "Yes, and you must be Festus." Then Hondo took a long, hard look, grinned, and asked, "Are you as disappointed as I am?"

Or the time he ran into former University of Texas schoolmate John Connally when the Connallys were living in the Governor's Mansion? "Hey, Hondo," the Governor said as they met at a Longhorn football game, "You still a goat-herder up there in the hills?" To which Hondo replied, "Yes, John, I sure am. What is it you are up to nowadays?"

Singer-songwriter Jerry Jeff Walker said it best, "That was Hondo's theatre in the real world."

As the self-appointed "Mayor of Luckenbach," Hondo loved an audience. He even upstaged comedian Bob Hope at a benefit for Fredericksburg's Nimitz Pacific War Museum in August, 1976. Hope was doing his monologue when out walked Hondo unannounced and handed him a note. After reading the note to himself, Hope doubled up with laughter. The note read, "Your fly is open." Then the Mayor of Luckenbach humbly spoke:

"Mr. Hope, sir, we of the Luckenbach Chamber of Commerce wanted to present you with a golf club but we don't play golf in Luckenbach. All we could find in the store was this here axe handle. Sorry it doesn't hav...e a head on it. You see, it's hard to get a head in Luckenbach." The crowd roared. "So," continued Hondo, "I'll just have to give you the *shaft*!" Hope was still laughing after Hondo presented him with a key to his city, a hairpin sprayed gold. "This will open any door in Luckenbach."

"Who writes your lines?" Hope asked Hondo after the show. "Oh, I just think 'em up my ownself," Hondo replied shyly with a shrug.

Another time, the Luckenbach Mayor made an appearance on a television talk show in Houston. Stumbling onstage, Hondo pretended to trip over cables and wires, falling flat on his face in front of the emcee's desk. Red-faced and panic-stricken, the show's host jumped to his feet. "Oh! Did you hurt yourself?" Brushing himself off with great dignity, Hondo responded, "No, but I sure smushed my crackers." Lifting a cellophane package of orange peanut butter crackers from his pocket, he said sadly, "Been savin' 'em so long." The audience loved him.

FREDERICKSBURG STANDARD

HONDO UPSTAGES BOB HOPE

At Luckenbach, Hondo had his own personal town to write about and be "Hondo" in. As "Peter Cedarstacker, Writer," he wrote his social satire for *The Comfort News*:

> *Luckenbach is a state of mind.*
>
> *Luckenbach is a free state. The present principality of Luckenbach was nearly a part of the United States but when the Washington politicians and statesmen came down to look over the proposed annexation they threw a whale of a stag party with the girls. In the commotion, they all signed what they thought was a deer huntin' lease and freed us. We've never been captured since. Ain't we lucky? Luckenbach is closed on Wednesday. "That's the day I sharpen scissors and separate nails in the general store," declared Hondo the Mayor. "On Thursday our army practices. We practice losin' so we can get foreign aid."*

To Tell the Truth

After Hondo and his partner Guich Koock bought the little antique town in 1970, it was ironic that Hondo traveled to New York to appear on the classic game show, *To Tell the Truth.* As a skilled storyteller, he would never spoil a good story with the truth. And it was up to you to sift fact from fiction.

Once onstage, the exquisite-looking white-bearded gentleman took his seat with the other two contestants, both imposters. The other two "Hondos" were tough Texan types, not unlike "Hoss" Cartwright on the TV western, *Bonanza. To Tell the Truth* host Garry Moore prompted the questioning. "Why did you buy the town?" panelist Peggy Cass asked the distinguished fellow in the black Western suit.

"Well," began the sober lie, "I tried to buy Dallas but it wasn't for sale. Clint Murchison wouldn't sell it."

He liked to change the story up. To some I'd heard him say, "I own a ranch in Fredericksburg and one in Sisterdale. Luckenbach was in between. Every evening when I'd go home from Sisterdale, I'd always stop in Luckenbach for a beer." Then to others, "I wanted Luckenbach for the same reason a dog buries a bone. So no other dog'll get it." Then I'd heard he wanted it because the store had the only double-decker wasp nest he'd ever seen and that sealed the deal.

The game show interrogation went on. The bearded fella with a twinkle in his eye and a black string tie gave answers that were so frustrating, wild or funny that he obviously stood out to them as a hired New York character actor—much too polished for the everyday owner of a tiny Texas hick town. What the panel didn't know was that it wasn't the owning of a town that was such a tall tale. It was that their subject, the owner himself, was a self-made master put-on artist whose wit, humor and colorful spirit knew no limits or stage.

The *To Tell the Truth* panel never could tell the truth. They were stumped and time had run out. "Would the real Hondo Crouch please stand up?" Garry Moore asked. Hondo, whom no one had bet on, stood up timidly, placing his cupped fingers over his mouth just like an embarrassed little boy who discovers he shouldn't have said what he did.

From a thank-you note received by Hondo from the entire staff on the show, I read that Hondo made "such a lasting impression on everyone" and gave them more pleasure for their minutes than anyone had in a long time. Even if they never really knew who the real Hondo Crouch was... and no one ever did. It would have been hard to ask the real Hondo Crouch to stand up. He never sat down.

"WHERE *in the* HELL *is* LUCKENBACH?"

I saw a youngster wearing a T-shirt that asked "Where in the hell is Luckenbach?" It's a tricky question.

Souvenir hunters are still stealing road and highway signs pointing our way even now, some 40 years after the hit song, "Luckenbach, Texas (Back to the Basics of Love)," came out. Back in '79, they almost loved the town to death by carrying off the store's signs, longneck beer bottles, even rocks. They even stole the old antique fire truck. If you would have asked Hondo where Luckenbach was located, you'd be frustrated with his various illusive tongue-in-cheek answers. Hondo didn't exactly want people to know. He protected it like all things he loved, including Texas.

"I always tell my Yankee friends, don't come to Texas," he would say. "It's terrible! Too hot, fleas in the sand, thorns, rattlesnakes!" His directions for getting to Luckenbach were vague at best: "Somewhere between Corpus Christi and Dallas."

One time he tried giving directions to a movie director. "Well, uh, I'll tell you. You get on I-10, go to 87, get off on 290, you know where that dead deer is in the ditch? Then you take a right on that farm-to-market road. You know, where that cattle guard is? And that mawkin' bird nest? Then

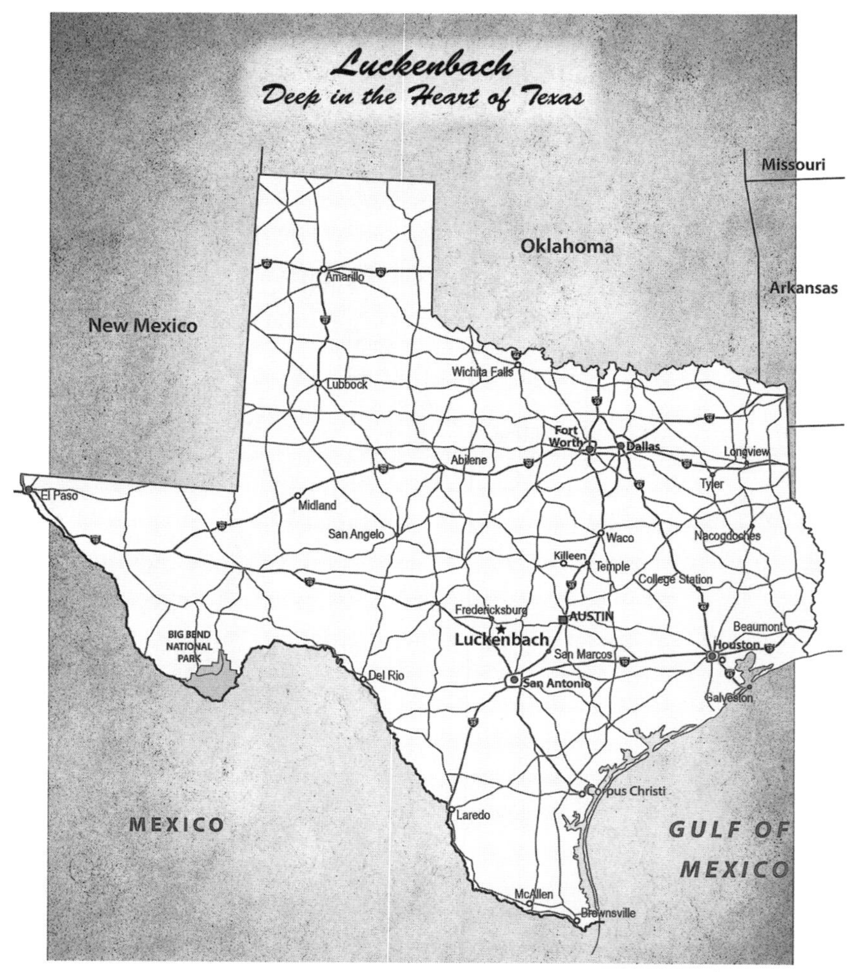

TEXAS ROAD MAP

take a left, go through a bump gate, two wooden gates, and a wire gap. Then you'll find Luckenbach in the canyon. No, well, it's more like a rut."

The director threw his hat down on the ground. "I'll be damned! Luckenbach must be at the end of the world!"

"Well, I'll be," Hondo hummed quietly, "I never thought of it *that* way. I thought you could *start* from here and go anywhere in the world!" Hondo continued, "We have discovered that Luckenbach, on the globe, is right in the middle of the world, and we figure if God hadn't intended for us to be in the center of the world, He wouldn't have put us there."

Hondo's partner, Guich Koock, proved this very contention by carrying a globe of the earth with him onto Johnny Carson's The *Tonight Show*. He put his finger and a string on the globe where Luckenbach was, wrapped the string around to meet at his finger. "See, Luckenbach is in the center of the Universe," said Guich. He explained further, "This discovery was the result of a science project of the Luckenbach boy who'd been in junior high the longest, and this is what he came up with."

In point of fact, Luckenbach is in Gillespie County, in the heart of what is known as the Texas Hill Country. It is 12 miles from Fredericksburg, the county seat. You can get there by heading east on Hwy. 290 and turning right on FM 1376. Pass Behrends Feed Store, pass Grapetown Road, and look for the Luckenbach Town Loop sign. Look to the right. It's hidden in the trees. You can't see it from the road.

If I'd wanted to give that kid in the T-shirt a history lesson, I might have informed him that the historic Pinta Trail of Central Texas, often called *El Camino Viejo*, or, The Old Road, ran right through Luckenbach. It was made by the feet of indigenous tribes and the hooves of their horses, hundreds maybe thousands of years ago, and expanded on by Spanish explorers in the 1700s. Its tracks were widened by wagons as it became the primary route of thousands of German immigrants during 1840–870, traveling from the Texas port of Indianola on Matagorda Bay, north to the Hill Country, crossing the Guadalupe River, on to Sisterdale and Luckenbach, and after crossing the Pedernales River, on to Fredericksburg.

The eastern branch of the Pinta Trail followed Luckenbach's present day FM1376, crossing South Grape Creek at Luckenbach itself. Grape Creek's flat limestone shelves and level flood plains at that spot made for easy fording; and easy flooding. Yes, I remember the Flood of July 2, 2002, when water filled up half of the general store, washed away the cotton gin and blacksmith shop, and the blacksmith anvil was found up in a cypress tree down FM1376. The Pinta Trail above Sisterdale remained partly in use until 1879 but soon thereafter was eclipsed by a road passing through Luckenbach on the way to Fredericksburg.

As Hondo said, "Funny, this li'l ol' place has been here 125 years and people are just now finding it."

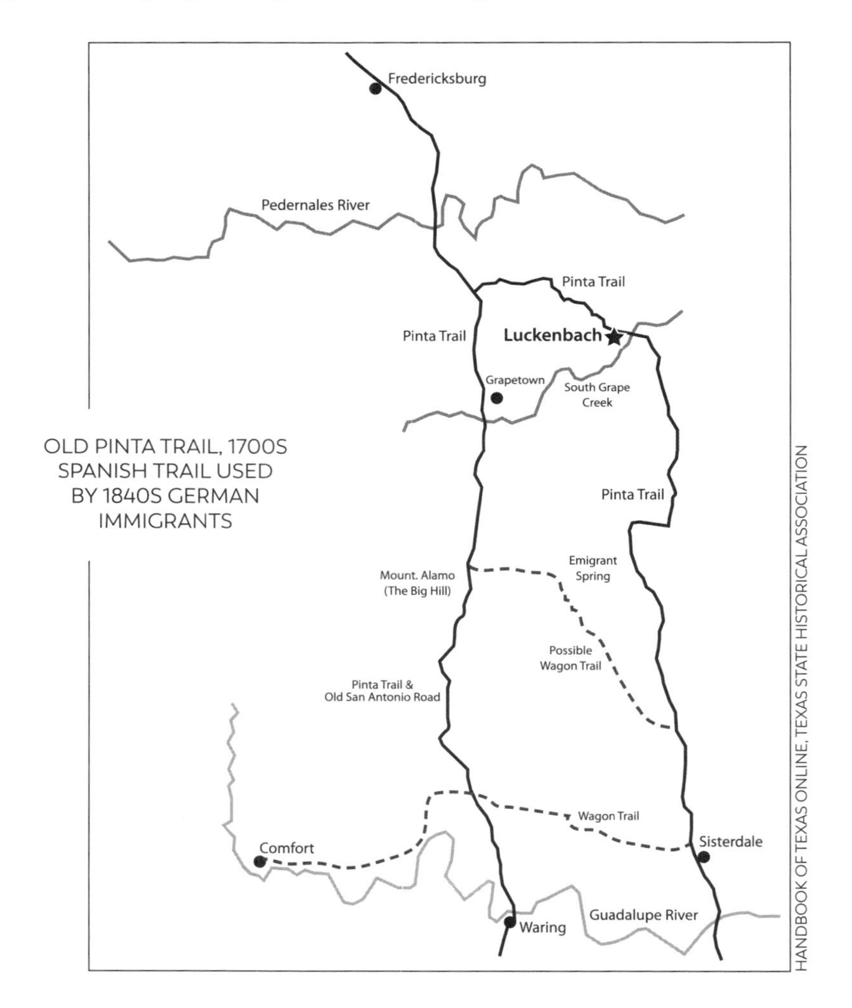

"IS LUCKENBACH *a* REAL TOWN?"

The other most-frequently-asked questions posed by tourists are, "Is Luckenbach a real town?" and "Is this it?"

"I always thought Luckenbach was a real town," the Texas State University student said at her bachelorette party. "Where's the McDonald's? There's not anything here!" Less is more in Luckenbach.

The community of Luckenbach is as old as the weather-beaten oak board Hondo hung above the store. Hondo had painted it with letters barely readable: "Oldest store in continuous operation I know of, I think—Moses, 1849."

In 1846, the village of Fredericksburg, only 12 miles away, was settled by Baron Otfried Hans Freiherr von Meusebach, head of the *Adelsverein*, a society of German noblemen appointed to colonize Central Texas. During this period, my forefathers played key roles in taming and developing the land by becoming among the first doctors, judges, land surveyors and ranchers in the region, in the process bringing the first fine wool sheep to the Hill Country.

As a marker dedicated by the Texas Historical Commission in 1986 notes, the little community of Grape Creek was started by

German immigrants and the Luckenbach family, who came here in the 1850s from Fredericksburg, settling along Grape Creek. The Grape Creek post office was operated briefly by William Luckenbach, its first Postmaster. Later, in 1886, Minna Engel, daughter of itinerant preacher August Engel, became Postmaster when she renamed the town "Luckenbach" after her husband, Albert Luckenbach.

Later, Albert and Minna moved on down the road and named another community "Albert," making for a grand total of two towns named in his honor. They traded with farmers as well as friendly Comanche Indians, with whom a peace treaty had been established. It was said to be the one unbroken Indian treaty in the history of the United States. I'll tell you about that later.

A year later, a dance hall was built and the post office established in the mercantile store building. A steam-operated cotton gin, now a rusty shell, was built in 1879 next to Grape Creek. Luckenbach's blacksmith shop was constructed the same year.

When the town's population pushed on up to 14, a combination school/church building was erected on another nearby road. The school, with an enrollment as high as 50 at one time, eventually consolidated with the Fredericksburg school district in 1967. The THC marker ends by adding: "John Russell 'Hondo' Crouch and others bought the town center in 1970 and promoted its rustic atmosphere."

"Let's Buy *a* Town"

"Hondo has some things that money can't buy:
Better go to Luckenbach and meet that guy..."

– "Everybody's Somebody in Luckenbach"
by Ted and Birdie Holliday

One morning in 1970, Guich Koock, a longtime family friend, who'd worked with Hondo at Camp Longhorn, appeared at our ranch house door with an ad from the *Fredericksburg Standard*, the local paper. The ad announced that Luckenbach was for sale. "Let's buy a town, Hondo!" Guich exclaimed.

"Well, my family had been coming to Luckenbach since I was just a child." Guich recalled. "We used to meet here for reunions. And Hondo, who ranches up the road, had been coming to Luckenbach for a good while, drinking beer. He was telling me one day that Mr. Engel, who had nobody in his family who was interested in running this little town, might want to sell it.

"So, I started talking with Mr. Engel, I guess about three years before we bought the town, but he wasn't ready to sell. Then one January morning we saw an ad in the Fredericksburg paper classified section, 'Town for Sale—Luckenbach, Texas.' The ad explained that the egg route would pay $60 a month for the town. So, we bought the town from Mr. Engel for $29,000. I don't know if it was 29, 19, or 12 acres. We never did get a close survey of the land. It included a pickup truck."

Benno Engel, direct descendant to Minna Engel and Albert Luckenbach, realized it was an end of an era. He had asthma real bad and couldn't wait on the customers, so he'd stay most of the time up front in the post office. He was postmaster here for years.

We used to ask him why he didn't hire somebody to help him with the bar, suggesting that some people might be waiting on themselves and then forgetting to pay. He said, "Well, maybe some of them are, but you know it's cheaper than hiring somebody."

The secret he didn't tell us, however, was that the post office was closing and that meant a big drop in customers.

"We could have a country store!" Mama encouraged Hondo and Guich. "Sell peaches, corn, tomatoes, squash...." Mama's face lit up when she talked about food.

Guich added, "It could be sort of a living museum. A revived Indian trading post."

Hondo was almost sold. "Yeah, it *does* have the only double-decker wasps' nest I've ever seen."

They all piled into the truck and went to talk to Benno. That day Benno sold Hondo a wooden flat of bright orange persimmons (Hondo hated persimmons) and, along with Guich, the town, but with a "lease with an option to buy." The deal was sealed in 1971.

Luckenbach's new owners walked through the general store's worn front door, which was covered in a collage of weathered FBI Most Wanted posters. Their eyes beheld century-old goods, dusty and caked with mud dauber wasp nests. A white line painted on the floor separated the saloon from the post office where thirty-seven families still collected their mail every week. While they traded overalls for eggs, they could also drink a cold one and swap news. Pointing to the line, Hondo warned, "You don't dare get caught drinking beer on the post office side."

Standing just inside the doorway, Hondo and Mama, my brother Juan and his wife Lulu, sister Cris, Guich and his wife Trish, looked the place over from rafters to worn linoleum.

Brooms, buckets, and new rope coils hung from the ceiling. Glass drawer bins held grains and staples. An octagonal cabinet with dozens of tiny drawers contained nails and bolts. Horseshoes

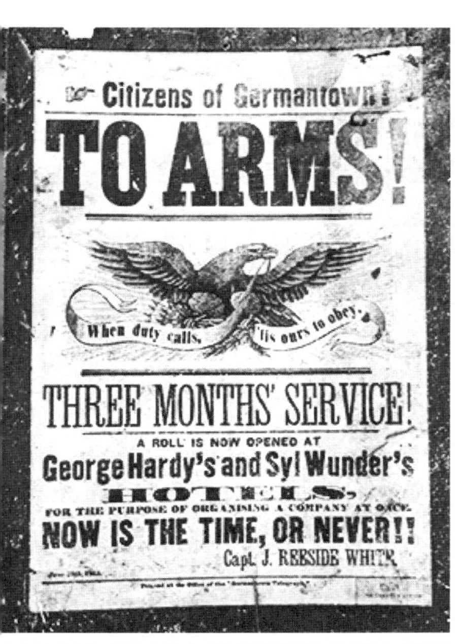

CALLING FOR HILL COUNTRY MILITIA, 1863

sold for 70 cents a pound, the horseshoe nails eight for a nickel. Galvanized washtubs, homemade soap, slop jars, harnesses, long underwear, homemade butter, spark plugs, a milk separator, coffee mill, and pepper mill added to the store's variety of merchandise.

Mama picked up a box of Red Man's Tea. "Nature's own cure for diseases rooted and imbedded in the blood," she read from the label. A child's casket rested up on the rafters. General stores back then also sold casket handles and embalming fluid. There was still a cardboard poster on the wall from 1863, calling for the Texas-Germans to sign up for the militia, to make sure they could keep their weapons.

I was in awe of generations of the rich history displayed in the bar and store; faded 1930 beer ads, fragile, dusty, everything held together by cobwebs. There's not a bar anywhere else in Texas that has more soul per square inch than Luckenbach's. It's actually our mall, the three-in-one building Hondo took to calling the Post Office-General Store-Beer Joint. Authenticity has a true heart. Old is beautiful. Pitiful and loving neglect is in.

The bar catered to simple, close-to-the-earth people, rural folk. Whoever enters the door is brought "back to the basics." Neither Bobby Emmons nor Chips Moman, who wrote "That Song," ever set foot in Luckenbach, but they got that much right.

Hondo and Guich looked things over in the saloon section. The area was top-heavy with countless moth-eaten deer head trophies. "So old," Hondo commented, "they were beginning to smile." Hondo

"LUCKENBACH SQUIRREL (TERRESTRIAL)" READS SIGN UNDER WATER BUFFALO

later added his Sierra Blanca eagle, mounted on the rafter over the bar, to the collection. Underneath the water buffalo head he placed a sign, "Luckenbach Squirrel—Terrestrial."

The walls were papered with ancient Coca-Cola and Pabst Blue Ribbon beer ads and a Jersey Crème Soda sign. A faded banner hung from the ceiling, a reminder of past *Schuetzenfests* (shooting fests) and *Saengerfests* (singing fests). A political sign touted "Ma Ferguson for Governor of Texas." Ma was in fact elected Governor. In 1925.

Focal point of the cozy saloon was a potbellied stove in the center of the room, placed in a sandbox. Undisturbed beneath the stove lay a hen. The hen nested there at peace throughout ensuing months of both quiet and busy days. When her chicks hatched, customers stepped aside as they scooted about.

A sign on the door read, "Henway for sale." A baited trap waiting for a customer to ask, "What's a Henway?" Hondo'd caught 'em: "'Bout three pounds."

Chickens seemed a natural part of the bar's life. We all remember Ruff the red alcoholic rooster. Hondo would amaze everybody by hypnotizing Ruff. He'd draw a white chalk line on the floor, hold Ruff's beak down on the line for a while, let go, and he'd stay there until you picked him up. Fed beer in bottle caps all day, by evening Ruff wobbled out the door just like the other customers. Too drunk to fly up into a limb to roost, it became bartender Sheriff Marge's last duty after locking up, to set Ruff up onto a limb to roost. "One night he fell outta the tree three times before he stayed!" Marge said.

When Hondo and Guich first bought the town, there were no flushing toilets, just a couple of outhouses scattered around. "Yes," Hondo told a reporter, "we plan to put in flushing toilets, but that's still in the planning stages." I remember when the new restroom was built and a pleasantly surprised woman came out of the Women's holding a warm, freshly laid egg in her hand. "Look what I found in the sink!"

What other bar can boast that their Executive Bartender, "Sheriff Marge" Mueller was a direct descendant of Luckenbach's first storeowner, Minna Engel, dating back to 1849? Marge, who passed away in 2004 at age 69, was born, raised and schooled in Luckenbach, and never left. She was known for her trademark long braids and rattlesnake earrings.

Marge remembered quieter days in the bar. There is an ice hole under the floor, now nailed shut with license plates. "There's a concrete box down there," she recalled. "Ice blocks were stored on wood shavings, covered with a tarp, and more wood shavings. People bought blocks of ice for their ice boxes and we also iced down the beer. Even in the summer, it'd last a week down there."

Another story about the store that we keep alive is the time during the historic drought of 1957, when a local farmer complained about the lack of rain and how hard it was to get a crop up. Some of his friends laughingly told him he wasn't paying the preacher enough. At church the following Sunday he gave the preacher two dollars, and before he made it back to the store in Luckenbach a cloudburst filled Grape Creek and sent water flooding the store. Wading through ankle-deep water he muttered, "You know, I think a dollar woulda been enough!"

The Luckenbach Regulars

Little bars like Luckenbach's were our country clubs for social show-and-tells. Everyone knew everyone, and all the gossip was better than reading the local newspaper. Luckenbach's bar customers and their stories are as rich as the décor and history. Where else can you have a captive audience for your deer hunting story, hear a genuine tall-tale or premiere a newly-written song without critique? I remember some special stories from Hondo. He treated us all like granddaddy long legs, with a thousand legs to pull.

The cozy bar is small, maybe 15' by 15'. "The wood stove used to be turned the other way," Marge remembered. "Hondo turned it to make more room. One time in the '20s, some drunk guy sitting on the bar fell off and broke his nose on the stove! Someone said, 'Let's take him to the doctor.' Someone else said, 'No let's just fix it right here and pull it straight.' So, they did and the guy never knew any different."

The "Regulars," or locals, were as ordinary yet colorful as characters in a movie. There was Oliver Ottmers, who raised chickens,

Roy Petsch, Jake Pehl and Travis Jenschke. Uncle Armond Engel walked down from his house every day and smoked his Salems. Tony Wilson looked like a movie star then. George Lovett and his "Warthog" van were always there. Mike O'Hare's feet were just healing up from a car wreck. Roberta, Marge's daughter, is still a regular. Horace "Manure" was considered the most obnoxious regular. *Cheers* had nothing on Luckenbach.

Singer-songwriter Rex Foster, Jr. came out from Comfort and camped out in a teepee on Grape Creek, shaking the cobwebs with his guitar playing for the benefit of the old domino players in the bar, and practicing in the dance hall with his band, "Rachel's Children." He was the first long-haired hippie to arrive, but far from the last.

Hondo and Roy Petch, a local chicken rancher, got involved in chicken talk one day. "I tried to raise 'em once." Hondo told Roy soberly, "but they kept dyin'. I dug neat little rows. Planted 'em with their heads stickin' up. They died." Roy was beginning to feel like a granddaddy long leg already. But he gave Hondo a respectful ear.

"So, I thought maybe I should plant 'em like bulbs, head down. They died too. So, then I wrote the Department of Agriculture and told 'em my problem. Do you know what they said?" he asked Roy in all seriousness. "Send a soil sample!"

No matter what grandiose venues Hondo would travel to for speeches or appearances, he never could impress the bar regulars back home. After returning from Washington D.C. with a group of colorful Texas characters for a Texas Folklife Festival he tried to brag at the bar. "Do you know where I've been?" he asked Travis Jenschke. "No, where?" "I've been to the Smithsonian Institution!" Travis looked at him unimpressed and with all honesty and said, "Golly, Hondo. Does Medicare pay for that?"

Porfie Cantu
–Number *One* Regular–

Luckenbach, Texas, Pop. 3, (as the tongue-in-cheek sign reads) means that this is a real town, but a town that is populated more by travelers than real residents.

Meet a real resident: Porfie Cantu and his wife Connie, one of "the three." His family has been living in Luckenbach since the '30s and is still here. Over the past seventy years they've seen a lot of changes. Their generations have subtly shaped the land around here as they have lived in quiet harmony amidst the not-so-quiet Luckenbach community.

There are other Luckenbach residents scattered near the school, the cemetery, and down country roads, out around oat fields. But the three houses in the Town Loop belong to the Benno Engels and the Cantu families. Porfie Cantu and his famous "push fiddle" accordion is part of the fabric of the eclectic Texas music produced by the pickers' circle that gathers regularly in the bar.

Porfie's grandfather, Vicente, a migrant worker from Mexico, was passing through this area in the '30s with his grandfather en route to work farms further north. Their car broke down, so this is where they stayed. Like most who find Luckenbach, it's either by accident or hard luck. They put down roots and set out making their own luck.

They bought a piece of land from the Engels for $700. Vicente and his son Pete, (Porfie's father) worked for the Bennie Luckenbachs, the Behrends and local families, chopping cedar, clearing brush and working the land you see around here.

Pete and his wife Dominga had eleven kids, Porfie being number eight. Porfie went to school in Fredericksburg, but his older brothers had gone to the Luckenbach School, before it closed in the '60s.

Nearly all of Dominga's babies were born at home. Connie, Porfie's wife, told how someone always ran to the store to call the doctor to come deliver them. "One time they even closed the store and took Dominga to the hospital for one of the births. Thank God she had all her babies before the store got that phone menu," she complained about the modern change. (The automated phone menu is when you are given options to press a number for your party).

The Cantu family especially remembers and misses the general store where they bought everything. "They had eggs, bread, fruits, groceries, and even ice in a metal ice box outside," recalled Connie. The kids came down for one-cent candies in a bag, the flavors of which took forever to decide. "We could always tell when Benito (Benno Engel) would put extra in the bag," Connie said. When Porfie was a boy, he made his candy money collecting and selling three-cent bottles in his little red wagon.

We don't see the Cantus much anymore, but I keep an indelible image of Porfie's father, Pete, in my mind from the time he came down to the store to fetch his wandering flock of turkeys. He fussed them home by cracking, not a bull whip, but a piece of garden hose. They minded him.

The main constant in Porfie's life has always been music. Talent runs in the family. Pete taught him to play the accordion, and his uncles and brothers are all self-taught musicians. Performing on stage since he was seven, Porfie has also been a professional drummer for ten years, and can play the electric bass. He is a prolific songwriter. Many still remember the song he wrote in 1963 about the assassination of JFK. It was played locally on the radio.

Porfie and family have always had a Christian band that still plays today in nondenominational Hispanic churches. He has written 22 gospel songs, which have been performed and recorded by other Latino artists. In the '80s he recorded nearly a dozen gospel albums that are played on Hispanic radio stations today.

Porfie and his "push fiddle" still squeeze out happy sounds with the Luckenbach regulars such as B.B. Morse (stand-up bass), Roger Moon (guitar and mule-skinner vocals), Bart Trotter and Kimbo (state champion fiddlers) and various washtub bass thumpers.

During one of his July Fourth Picnics at Luckenbach, Willie Nelson had invited Porfie to play on stage with him and Little Joe y La Familia's band, but he never did. Instead, he preferred to walk across the creek and stand backstage, next to the president of *The Wall Street Journal*, to listen to the 12-hour concert, free. Porfie didn't play on stage with Willie, but he did get to sing "Jalisco," sitting with Hondo on the big log bench under the oak trees he fondly remembered.

Juan *and* Ken: *The* Luckenbach Air Force "Thirty Seconds *Over* Luckenbach"

There's been some amazing activity in the skies of Luckenbach over the years, dating back to Jacob Brodbeck's spring-powered flying machine that went aloft near Luckenbach in 1865, fully 39 years before the Wright Brothers got off the ground.

Another time, a helicopter landed on the field one day just to "go out to eat" at the hamburger stand. My daring brother, Juan Crouch, jumped out of a crashing helicopter in Viet Nam and lived to tell about it. When he came home, he crash-landed

CAPT. KEN MORGAN AND THE LUCKENBACH LUFTWAFFE

his 1949 Luscombe airplane in a nearby field at Luckenbach and lived to tell about that, too. The vertical tail stabilizer fell off. He had purchased the aircraft from another of Luckenbach's partners, Capt. Ken Morgan, retired Continental Airlines pilot, husband of Kathy Morgan, who became a partner in Luckenbach along with Guich and Hondo.

But it was in 1979 that this strange incident occurred that involved the Cantus and my brother Juan, a story I am embarrassed to relay. There are some of us who are content to spend our spare time in more boring, legal, less dangerous ways.

Juan kept his '49 Luscombe plane at his Block Creek Ranch in Sisterdale, as did his friend John Schuh, who flew a 1969 Cessna 150, and they decided to go flying one day. By the time they took off from the ranch and climbed, they were already over Luckenbach. Of course, they didn't file a flight plan because then they'd only be allowed to fly no higher than 500 feet. They needed 2500 feet for this game which they had in mind to work.

Juan, at 33, was the same age as his 1946 Luscombe, barnstormed in the skies over Luckenbach with his daredevil compadre, 19-year-old stunt pilot John. Their game involved throwing out a roll of toilet paper, and taking turns to clip and cut the flying paper into as many pieces as possible before it hit the ground. The little cardboard cylinder at the end of the roll acted as a kite's tail so the long threads of paper could dance in the air.

The dog fighters swarmed dangerously behind one another in order to cut up the paper with propeller or wing into at least five pieces.

Alarmed, Porfie's father, old man Pete Cantu, frantically called the sheriff and said, "There's two airplanes chasing each other and they're throwing their drugs out, all this white stuff, and it's landing on our property!" The police quickly responded but couldn't find anything.

"Do you have a ladder?" the officers asked. "No," said Pete. They had to go round one up somewhere. When they climbed on to the roof, they asked, "Is this it?" holding up the toilet paper. "Yes, that's it!" exclaimed Pete. From that day on, Pete had painted CANTU in five-foot letters on his roof to prevent any further unusual bombings from the air.

Zip Zimmerman –*Outlaw* Security

For some-odd 30 years one of Luckenbach's most beloved icons and "peacekeeper" was Zip Zimmerman, Luckenbach's One-Man Homeland Security. Zip's motto isn't "Everybody's Somebody" but rather, "Everybody's Everything in Luckenbach." He has done everything—bounced, bartended, substitute managed, carpentered, driven his truck and flatbed in every parade, and protected us from riots during many mass gatherings—from three up to 13,000 people. Bottom line: Don't mess with Zip. His huge action-hero figure is intimidating. I've always wanted to beat on his barrel chest to see if it echoes.

"The best cops have criminal minds," confessed Zip, referring to his rebellious youth in Mason, Texas. "But really, I'm real easy going and I like everybody. The secret to my success has always been how you approach people and how you talk to them. Makes all the difference in the world."

In 1976, Zip came from Mason to live at Luckenbach, sleeping in his '61 GMC truck for eight months. He literally awoke during Hondo's wake under the neighboring oak trees. His day job was carpentering at the nearby LBJ Ranch, while working weekends at Luckenbach. Zip helped Sheriff Marge serve beer in the bullpen and bounced the dances. Zip bathed in the tin bathtub that was still in the Egg House (which served as the "mayor's" office), with a garden hose stuck through the window to fill it up.

In '76, beer was 55 cents. There were no cash registers and money was stashed in cigar boxes or a wooden drawer under the bar. There was no night bank depository in Fredericksburg at the time, so Zip used the money bag as a pillow as he slept in his truck bed. He kept a .22 single-shot by his side in case of a robbery attempt. Sometimes it rained on him he said, but after 2:00 a.m. who cared? Kathy Morgan, Ken's wife, would come by in the morning to get the money bag.

"We used to put money in the ice hole," Zip said. The 1850-era ice hole, which is no longer there, was a hinged secret door in the floor of the bar; just a dirt hole with some hay.

"We actually put ice in there for a big event, like the World's Fair. This was before the purchase of the walk-in cooler. I'd go to the Deluxe or Bill's Ice House," Zip said, "and get five or six 500-pound blocks of ice. This was real ice, not aeriated. I would put it in the back of my truck, uncovered, and drive to Luckenbach without it melting." It was chipped and put into big bathtub bins for the beer.

Things weren't always calm. In Zip's kind of work, time is either eventless and boring or too exciting and dangerous. Back in the '70s, things could be wild and wooly.

Take for instance the time Zip was bouncing at a dance and Tom Joy pulled a pistol. It resulted in the biggest shoot-out in Luckenbach history.

"It all started," Zip reported, "When this guy (Tom) kicked George Lovett in the balls." Zip held Tom in a full-nelson wrestling hold on the ground until the other hired guards could come help him. Every time Tom would raise his head Zip bopped it back down, causing it to hit the pavement, later requiring 55 stitches.

When the guards ran up to help, they grabbed Zip instead, before they realized who the real bad guy was. Zip finally got Tom into his truck. Then Tom pulled a gun, and Zip shoved Kar-en (now his eight-months pregnant wife) out of the way, yelling to the guards, "He's got a piece!"

Zip grabbed Tom Joy's left arm, which was holding the gun. "I was trying to break his arm," Zip said. Joy got two shots off in the air.

"Watch your eyes!" warned the other security guard, who had a shotgun. Zip turned his head in the nick of time as the guard fired his shotgun twice—dead center towards the windshield. Glass scattered everywhere. Tom Joy stormed outta town only to make it to the KOA campground about five miles away before his engine blew up.

Deputy Sheriff Sonny Grobe, always the one to come out to Luckenbach for trouble calls, came out to investigate the reason for Tom's bloody head.

"I never hit him," Zip told him, "I was just keeping him to the ground in a full-nelson hold."

"I figured there was another side of this story," Grobe said. Zip had to go in front of a grand jury for his part in the shoot-out. Joy was indicted for attempted murder and given 15 years' probation. "Things got a little western then," Zip laughed. "We've got everyone trained now."

Zip, being in his line of work, knew all the hot local hangouts, like the 87 Drive In, the Luckenbach bar and the Tower. He heard all the police stories and bar gossip.

One story concerned Beansie Rausch, a rancher in nearby Sisterdale. "The funniest story I remember," laughed Zip, "was when Beansie Rausch was at the 87 Drive In. Beansie was always pulling a big trailer of stock around, either buying or trading. While he was inside the 87 flirting with a woman, the husband of the woman was letting out all of Beansie's cattle from his trailer. They were runnin' all over the place. Every man and deputy sheriff in town was trying to herd them down Highway Street towards the auction!"

Zip couldn't end the bar/police stories without mentioning Sheriff Hugo Klaerner and Sheriff Milton Jung. Udo Klaerner, Hugo's father, was sheriff before him. "Udo had arrested a black gal for hot checks and gave her 30 days in jail," Zip recounted. "She told the deputies she needed to see the sheriff. When Udo Klaerner was brought to her cell she said, "Mr. Sheriff, I want a box of Kotex." Udo frowned, then defiantly answered, "Young lady, you'll eat Post Toasties like the rest of the prisoners!" Sometimes the German-English speaking sheriffs didn't understand everything.

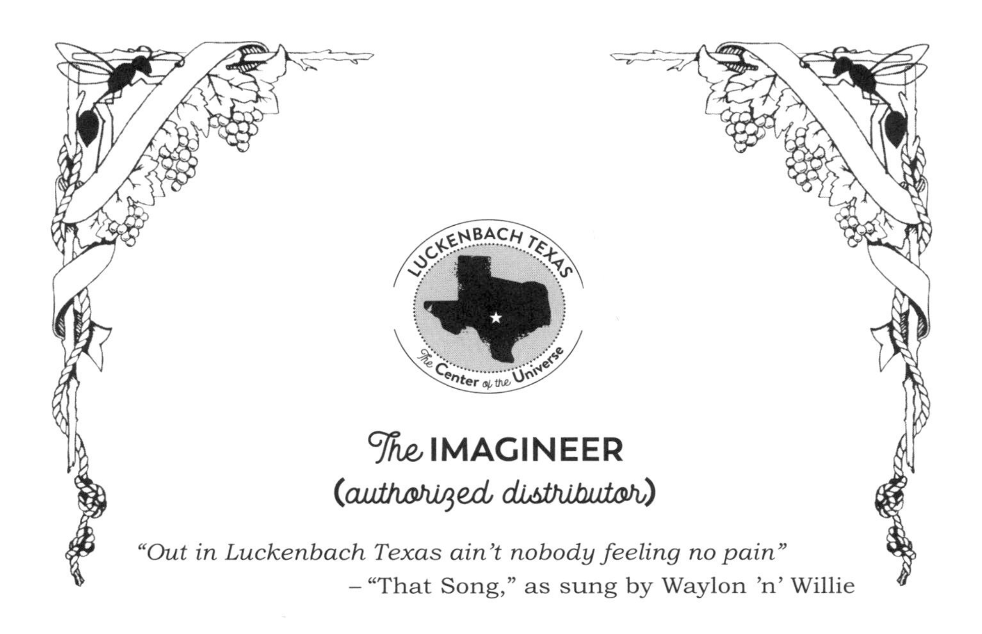

The IMAGINEER (authorized distributor)

"Out in Luckenbach Texas ain't nobody feeling no pain"
– "That Song," as sung by Waylon 'n' Willie

Fredericksburg donated the town's only parking meter, which Hondo installed in front of the dance hall. "I'm responsible for the only accident in Luckenbach," confessed the Mayor. "That parkin' meter caused a three-car pileup. It worked so well when I first put it up. All the little ladies put pennies in it. They thought it was a slot machine. A tourist came by and put a whole dime in it. The parkin' meter could hardly digest it! Never had a dime before. It even smoked a little. All the guy did was walk across town (aka, the street), got a drink, came back, and left. Well, he left so much free time that three guys jumped in their pickups and tried to use it up. Caused the only three-car pileup in 125 years!"

By December of 1972, Luckenbach acquired a third partner, Kathy Morgan. She and her husband Ken, a pilot for Continental Airlines, had moved from California to Blanco, Texas, in 1968.

Deciding that activities at the store could help fill her days, Kathy brought more capital into the partnership and a lot of spit and polish to the store. Fresh wildflowers sometimes bloomed from

HECK/HILLIARD

THE NEW OWNERS: GUICH KOOCK, KATHY MORGAN, HONDO

a mason jar on the counter. She sewed folk shirts and dresses for the store's nonexistent ready-to-wear department. Ken soon became one of Hondo's best friends.

The lights of Hollywood dazzled Guich's eyes not long afterward. He eventually left the partnership and egg route to enter a singing cowboy contest and, quickly finding movie roles in *American Ninja* and 1974's *Sugarland Express*. He brought fellow *Sugarland Express* cast members Goldie Hawn and Ben Johnson and first-time director Steven Spielberg out to Luckenbach. Later, he was a regular on the TV series *Carter Country*. Nevertheless, he continued to return periodically to stage his favorite event, the "Luckenbach Great World's Fair."

Four weeks after my family bought the town, we were surprised to find that the government was closing down the post office in its sweeping postal cutback. This was a little secret Benno hadn't told us. Hondo wrote a futile plea on April 1, 1971, to Senator John Tower. "We know how to preserve old buildings, customs, long underwear and Argo starch," Hondo explained, "but could you give any information, help or instructions on the preservation of post offices?"

SAN ANTONIO EXPRESS NEWS

GOLDIE HAWN VISITS HONDO AT LUCKENBACH

Its closing brought about a sharp decline in grocery sales. Now our customers went to Fredericksburg for their mail and goods. The tavern's patrons and egg customers remained loyal, however. It became a disappointment to Mama that the character of the place was transforming from a country store to a beer joint.

Hondo made a joke out of losing the post office. "I feel like I'm really responsible for the post office closing down," he'd apologize to people, "because I'm so conservative. It's my fault, really. But I just couldn't see why I should send off a BIG mail sack with one little letter down in the bottom so lonesome. I kept it 'til it got full. Took seven months." Now Guich's and Hondo's creative minds started swirling. They'd have to think up something to keep people coming.

Since the closing of the post office, the zaniest festivals imaginable took place for the remaining six years of Hondo's life. In an effort to produce income, there arose the Women's Only Chili Cook-off, the Great Luckenbach World's Fairs, the Hug-Ins, the Return of the Mud Dauber, and the Non-Buy-Centennial, to name a few. Hondo's calling card said, "Imagineer—authorized distributor."

Hondo and Kathy Morgan were afraid to bring the public out to their little lazy, fragile town. We heard Kathy say, "We don't mind people dropping by Luckenbach, as long as they're not customers. Customers always want something." Of the six permanent residents in Luckenbach, Hondo said, "We're gonna have a population explosion if we're not careful." He'd jokingly explain the census always staying at three to six by saying, "Every time a baby's born in Luckenbach, a man leaves town."

The Ladies-Only Chili Bust

The first bit of excitement to vibrate Luckenbach's cobwebs was the October 16, 1971 staging of the Susan B. Anthony Memorial Chili Cook-off.

Hondo claimed he'd always wanted to have a woman's chili cook-off in Luckenbach where the ladies could cook chili and show off where nobody'd see 'em. Hondo described this event as "a women's chili cookin' contest where you make one little lady happy and 500 mad."

Chili cook-offs in Texas originated as annual events in the West Texas ghost town of Terlingua in 1967, but were open to male contestants only. Hondo came to the rescue and formed a "Hell Hath No Fury (Like a Woman Scorned) Society" to demand the ladies be allowed to cook. He said he'd "always wanted to hold a 'Ladies Chili Bust'."

For the next 33 years, the cook-offs were always named after Texas female icons or national heroines. The first one was in honor of Susan B. Anthony. Other various honorees were Amelia Earhardt, Governor Ma Ferguson, Queen Nefertiti, Hallie Stillwell, Annie Oakley, Jane Long, Adina De Zavala, Clara Driscoll, Henrietta King, Molly Goodnight and Dale Evans, to name a few.

Thanks to the termites, which ate through a box of keepsakes on my closet floor, I ran across the very first couple of press

1985 POSTER OF 15TH ANNUAL WOMANS ONLY CHILI BUST HONORING JANE LONG.

releases for the Women's-Only Chili Busts in '71 and '72. The First Annual World Renowned Women's International Chili Bust was announced from the little principality of Luckenbach like this:

> *The LCC (That's short for Luckenbach Chamber of Commerce, to save space) met at the Luckenbach beer joint-post office, Monday of this week. When Mrs. Worstbottom, President, stands up and waves a beer bottle, brother, the meetin' has come to order, and it's official.*
>
> *"If the men can go to Terlingua, the girls can come to beautiful downtown Luckenbach." We decided that with a vote. Took one case of beer. Also voted not to stare at the tourists. Mrs. Worstbottom, President, would like to take this chance to invite all the women in the world to Luckenbach for the "Women's Chili Bust", October 16 1971.*

And in 1972, the second Chili Bust press release read like this:

> *The Women's Liberation movement in Texas will reach its highest point so far on October 28 when Hondo Crouch, Foreign Minister of Luckenbach, Texas holds the Second First Annual Amelia Jenks Bloomer Chili Cook-In for Women Only. The women are still barred from most chili cook-offs and even resorted to picketing at the San Marcos Chilympiad. 'Might as well let 'em prove again this year whatever it was they proved last year,' Hondo said. If you get to looking for Luckenbach that day and can't find it, follow a farmer. He'll be on his way to the fun in the metropolitan section of the downtown area of Luckenbach.*

For the first women's chili cook-off, all twenty-one entries were acknowledged upon receipt by a personal handwritten letter from Hondo and Guich on a brown paper sack outlining the day's schedule of events. Unmentioned were the horseshoe and washer pitching, the soap-making demonstrations, and the flea market. There was even talk of a "Miss Luckenbach" contest to select the most beautiful female hound dog.

Oct. 10, 1971

Dear Lady Chili Cook:

Thank you for your entry... the itinerary looks something like this:

9:00 a.m. - Contestants begin arriving
10:00 a.m. - Contestants still arriving
11:00 a.m. - To be announced
12:00 noon - Something
1:00 p.m. - More
3:30 p.m. - Judging of chili by Judges
5:00 p.m. - Prizes awarded to winners
6:00 p.m. - To be announced
9:00 p.m. - Big Dance

Each contestant will need to bring everything (EVERYTHING!) needed to cook, hold, prepare, taste, stir, etc. the chili.

We are eagerly anticipating this great historical event and appreciate your interest and participation in this giant step for woman-kind.

Til October 16 —-
Guich Koock, Premier
and Hondo Crouch, Foreign Minister and Mayor

Three judges had been imported from "Far-off places." Mary Faulk Koock, Guich's mother and renowned food authority, came from her restaurant, Green Pastures, in Austin; from the *Austin American-Statesman* came columnist Nat Henderson; George White came all the way from the Dallas Cowboy Chili Parlor in New York to complete the trio.

Showmanship was the biggest part of the contest. A real covered wagon with a chuck wagon box on back showed up. The women from Fredericksburg all cooked on cast iron Dutch ovens and skillets over fires on the ground. At the last minute, Trish Koock and Lulu Crouch ran into Fredericksburg and bought a rhinestone crown at Keunemann's Dry Goods, returning just as the judges had settled on Cindi Craig's "Jersey Lily" chili for first place. "Allegani Jani" Schofield won second place with her "Hot Pants Chili." A group of five University of Texas coeds tied for third place, while Frank Horlock's (who was the Chairman of the Board of Pearl Brewery) black maid from Houston, took home a prize for her recipe, "Dark Horse Chili."

That night everyone danced to the toe-tapping music of Felix Pehl and Sheriff Hugo Klaerner's oompah band. Hugo, Fredericksburg's 250-pound sheriff, usually played a tuba. That night, however, he played the trumpet because he had to leave the bandstand at intervals to check on maintaining the peace on Luckenbach's only street, and it was too much effort to get unwrapped from the tuba each time.

There was no trouble. It was the largest crowd ever gathered up to that point at Luckenbach, but it was only the first of many successive record-breaking crowds. For the last Chili Bust in 2004, Hondo's niece, Mary Lee Edwards, drove up in her Jaguar to donate the last chili queen's crown, an antique gold one.

Cedar Creek Clippings

Chili Wars

October 21, 1971

(Dear Editor, I'm writin' this at Trapper Gutowsky's house. I broke my pencil and he won't let me take his out of the house.)

Things are kinda quiet 'round Luckenbach since the Ladies Chili Bust was held. Nearly everybody who cared went home.

The winnin' chili was called "Jersey Lilly Chili". Then there was "Hot Pants Chili", "Dark Horse", "Javelina Hash", and "Rocket Chili", a bowl would make you take off.

There was only one fight all day long, and that was between two lady chili cookers over whose chili was the best. It all started when one flipped a piece of chili at the other. It was returned, different brand. Then a small handful caught the lady with the tobacco-colored hair on the cheek, eye too. It was returned with gusto. Tempers flared. A big handful was then generously traded, followed by pots of chili to the body. Both turned jalapeno green. When the hair pullin' started we all threw 'em in the creek by the Park Side Road for them to cool off. They did.

One got so cold she said, "I'm shiverin' like a Chilly Queen." The other one thought she was smartin' off and smacked her one.

A woman's chili cookin' contest is where you make one little old lady happy and 500 mad. (I gotta go. The rats are climbin' 'round on Trapper's phone like they want to use it.)

Peter Cedarstacker
Writer

Remember: Fight tardiness..... procrastination

"The mystery and the history is what people loved about these crazy chili cook-offs at Luckenbach. It was so out in the boonies and such a primitive place, (bringing your own firewood and water) it made people forget where they came from and huddle closer together," said one of the contestants.

The first women's chili bust started with 21 entries and 32 years later, it ended with 70. The chili cook-offs evolved into great fraternal chili-centric groups called PODs, like the Houston POD and Chili Appreciation Society International. At the height of "chili madness," the late Hal John Wimberly published the *Goat Gap Gazette*, a newsletter that chronicled big doings in the chili world. A memorial campfire ring is named and dedicated to him at Luckenbach, the heart and soul of chili heads, which has become a coffer for the ashes of other "fraternity members" as well.

BRYAN HECK

ALLEGANI JANI'S "HOT PANTS CHILI"

Terlingua

Hondo accompanied his top two winners- the Horlock's black maid's "Dark Horse Chili" and Allegani Jani's "Hot Pants Chili,"—to the World Championship in Terlingua (meaning "three tongues" in Spanish), a forsaken ghost town out in the West Texas desert, where contestants from all over the nation gathered for the popular Texas frolic. Allegani Jani, who would win the World's Chili Championship, noticed the media following her everywhere. The feminist movement in America was strong that year and CBS sent a crew from the sports department down to follow them around.

The whole idea of chili cook-offs started out as a farce, a joke. The farce became an idea, the idea an excuse for zaniness. It was like spring break for adults.

Here's a brief history: Frank X. Tolbert and Wick Fowler, both writers for the *Dallas Morning News*, cooked and talked a lot about chili (Wick went on to develop the famous Two-Alarm brand). The Chili War broke out when they heard of a New York Yankee, H. Allen Smith (a humorist writer for *Holiday* magazine) claiming he knew more about chili than anyone else in the world. To the Texans, this was rank heresy of the vilest order and they issued a challenge to Smith to compare bowls of red, *mano a mano*.

Terlingua was chosen the battle ground to settle the issue because it was remote, neutral, and owned by a man named David DeWitt.

The epic confrontation was judged by DeWitt, former San Antonio mayor Maury Maverick and Halley Stillwell, the oldest, only woman judge/rancher in Brewster County, the largest county in Texas, where Terlingua was located. David DeWitt's taste buds got burned out, so the fight was declared a draw between Wick and the Yankee interloper. Terlingua, to this day still has the National Championship Cook-off each November.

Gordon Fowler, Wick's son, said, "I first met Hondo in '68 at a chili cook-off in Terlingua as he was taking Rocky Caliche to the doctor in Alpine after being blown up by gunpowder." Rocky had thrown gunpowder into the fire for special effects as Hondo was cooking either his "Armadillo Chili on the Half Shell," or famous "Lost by a Hare" rabbit stew.

"Those were the days," Gordon reminisced, "when chili cook-offs were still fun, before too many rules and seriousness. We even pre-engraved trophies with the names of the guys who we wanted to win. Now, competition is as stiff as NASCAR racing."

Hondo's cook-off showmanship was more "show" than "cook." Surrounded by rusty traps and cans, Dutch ovens, and twenty pounds of deer and cow bones, with sausage, herbs, and condiments spread out on an Indian blanket and labeled "Secret" and "Confidential," Hondo stirred his chili in a dried armadillo shell, which once served as our Easter basket.

His nearby sign "Stand Back—Chili Happening" was a gentle warning. He actually used gunpowder to sprinkle in the fire for an occasional blast. As Gordon Fowler related, it accidentally fell into the fire, exploding in the face of Hondo's cooking partner, Rocky Caliche, so nicknamed by Hondo because he worked for the highway department. He was taken to a gas station/café at Study Butte for medical attention. "He's young, he'll heal fast, ya know," Hondo assured the crowd. Hondo said he was disqualified by the judges, however, because he was cooking *pure* "Armadiller Chili," and "they happened to find a *rabbit* hair in it! I lost by a hare!" he exclaimed.

Hondo's Terlingua Armadiller on the Half Shell recipe:

ONE Medium armadillo
Other stuff
Save the shell

Dice armadillo into chunks, do not grind. Next, dye them pea green to produce the color for Green Chili. Use only "Ysleta Red" chili pods, grown only in Ysleta because the sod is peculiar. Grind three comino seeds vigorously. Add jigger of tequila, pinch of salt, slice of lime. (May be either taken internally or added to chili.) For chili thickening, put in a raw egg, two if they're cheap. And if you can borrow some, add olive oil. It's too expensive to buy. Add green onion tops and finely ground cedar bark. Sprinkle with green spinach or fresh watercress and serve on the half shell.

ARMADILLO CHILI ON THE HALF SHELL AT TERLINGUA

His armadillo recipe, whose main ingredient was tongue-in-cheek, now resides for posterity in the archives of the Institute of Texas Cultures in San Antonio. The Imagineer of Luckenbach, more widely known than ever before, was being put under a public magnifying glass for scrutiny as his popularity among the masses—and the media—grew.

The Terlingua chili cookers traditionally trekked across the Rio Grande to the nearby border town of San Carlos, in the neighboring

Mexican state of Chihuahua. One day I showed Gordon Fowler Hondo's guitar from one of those excursions; the guitar had a bullet hole in it. "Knowing Hondo, he probably put that hole there to make a good story," I confessed to Gordon. "No, he didn't," Gordon said. "I know that guitar and I gave it to him."

The legendary guitar was found in the tiny border town of San Carlos (like Luckenbach, Population 3), in what we used to call "Old Mexico." It used to be a tradition for visitors to the area to visit the San Carlos town bar by either wading or riding across in a boat. A donkey waited to carry customers into town. "It was like entering a Clint Eastwood movie set," remembered Gordon. "We tied our donkey up at the saloon."

Hondo, Mayor of Luckenbach, met David, the Presidente (or mayor) of San Carlos. "What happened to him?" Hondo asked, pointing to the town drunk, Emilio, who was on crutches with a bandaged leg. "Got shot playing the guitar—over a woman," David explained. A .38 bullet went through the guitar and the leg, both.

Intrigued by the story and not ready to believe someone was pulling his leg, Hondo asked to see the guitar. Mayor David sent Emilio limping to retrieve it. Gordon wanted to buy the relic. Sensing that it was already something special, Emilio declared that the asking price was $200.00. After a photo was made of Gordon, Hondo, Emilio and the guitar, Gordon gave the guitar to Hondo. Like Willie's guitar, Trigger, there was much pick damage from miles of playing. Aside from the bullet hole, the word "*Recuerdo*" ("I remember") was carved into it. The unplayed quiet guitar that now hangs in my house where it continues to sing of true love and love gone wrong. Images that linger longer than we will.

On May 11, 2013, the traditional Terlingua chili group met down at the border village of Lajitas, on the U.S. side not far from Terlingua, in a grand Texas (which means "friendship") style public relations gesture. The memorable event was called *Voices from Both*

PAT O'BRYAN

VOICES FROM BOTH SIDES OF THE RIO GRANDE RIVER

Sides, and was made up of friends and neighbors of Lajitas and Mexico, gathering on both sides of the river.

Maggie Montgomery and the Luckenbachians told the story: “We serenaded Mexico from the Lajitas side and they serenaded us from the other side in return. First border party in over ten years, since the informal crossings that had been a tradition for many decades were officially prohibited after 9/11. A totally magic and very touching day! We shared food and music from both sides; tacos from their side and brisket from our side and beer from both sides.”

All pretenses and ordinances were drowned when the Mexican mayor, who was called “El Presidente,” gave a speech, put down the microphone and started wading across the river to meet dignitaries from the Lajitas side. They met in the middle and shook hands and then embraced.

Uproarious cheers and shouts of “*Viva*!” erupted from both sides. Then out came the Frisbees and hula hoops and all the children, dogs and grownups were in the water meeting in love and friendship. The atmosphere was full of celebration and joy. This happening is destined to be an annual event. We formed a human bridge across the water. (Better than a wall).

Much love and thanks to Anita and George Goss for their hospitality to the Luckenbach contingency: Allegani Jani, Patrick Smith and Maggie Montgomery. They opened their home and hearts to us and introduced us to many of the Big Bend pickers. It reminded us of Luckenbach, with so much talent and love and friendship. We'll be back next year or sooner to do it all over again! *Viva* Terlingua!

The Luckenbach Great World's Fair

There were four Luckenbach Great World Fairs: '73, '74, '77 and '81. The first one was held from June 29 to July 1, 1973. Hondo and Guich, the main organizers, were assisted by Wally Pryor, Igor Loving, and PR man Jack Harmon. Ten thousand came. Freaks, straights, rednecks, businessmen; the whole spectrum of humanity was represented. "People were as thick as yellow jackets in a nest," Hondo commented. In the next two years the fair had to be held in Fredericksburg so Luckenbach could escape being trampled into extinction.

A hundred artists and craftsmen set up booths. There were soap-making demonstrations. Sugar cane was ground down for molasses-making in Luckenbach's existing fire pit. Woodcarving and horseshoeing skills were displayed. Mexican *charros* performed. Contests involving frontier skills such as musket shooting took place. Hondo won the tobacco spitting contest.

MARY LEE EDWARDS

ARMADILLO RACES

MARY LEE EDWARDS

BOY WAITING HIS TURN WITH ARMADILLO

Other contests included chicken flying, cow chip throwing (a semi-skill) and armadillo races. Charley Loving, who was in charge of the Wright Brothers Chicken Flyin' Contest, was asked why they picked chickens to fly. The answer was, "Pigs are too hard to load in mailboxes" (which were re-purposed as poultry race chutes).

The Cannon Shootin' Contest was the big hit of the celebration. The cannoneers had real cannons. Back then you could find a real cannon on any courthouse lawn. The target was a wooden outhouse on the banks of Snail Creek. The cannon "balls" which were expelled out of cannons at high velocity were mostly beer cans filled with concrete. They lacked accuracy. Tony Bell, however, the acknowledged star, had found a supply of iron cannon balls that were deadly accurate.

LARRY UPSHAW / *TEXAS HIGHWAYS*

GRINDING SUGAR CANE AT HE MOLASSES PRESS

Soldiers marched and Kiowa Indians from Oklahoma danced down Luckenbach's only street, all two hundred feet of it. Guich was unshirted, ridden into town on a horse, and then "tarred and feathered" with molasses and pillow feathers, by a couple of rough women who resented being asked to do menial chores like pick up beer cans and evict drunks.

Augustine Lopez from Fredericksburg had rounded up the fattest diamondback rattlers for his chicken-fried rattlesnake steaks. You could walk up to the glass cage and pick your snake. "Rattlesnake meat provides certain vitamins not ordinarily found in the everyday diet of most Americans," Lopez announced. "It is perfectly proper to eat rattlesnake with the fingers."

That mid-afternoon, Saturday, my sons Ren and Kit ran screaming to me when they heard gunshots fired. A body rolled off the dance hall roof and almost landed on the parking meter. Before we could tell what was happening, the street suddenly cleared and three gunmen, as if in a scene from *The Wild Bunch*, stalked into town.

From the opposite direction strode the "bad guys." They took their stance, drew their guns, and "shot it out," falling hard when "hit." The "Hole-in-the-Wall" professional gunfighters had made their entry into Luckenbach. "Fist fights," which sometimes actually drew blood, would send them sprawling into the dust, after which they'd get up, dust themselves off, slap each other on the back, and go have a cold beer under the live oaks. While sitting there swapping jokes, they might get into another fracas and the dust would fly again. Ren followed them around all day, fascinated. They staged shoot-outs every few hours in the street. Couldn't do that again now!

As usual, the stage just seemed to get under Hondo. He loved his theater live, in the real world, slapstick and spontaneous. Dressed in a black wig, top hat, and buffalo robe, he pretended to be a tourist with his dusty Brownie box camera. He'd get right between the fighters, who'd knock him down every time. Or he'd nonchalantly carry a cardboard tray of empty beer cans through the street, throwing them high into the air and falling face down in the dust when he'd hear a shot. By day's end he had "died" about four times and was dusty from head to foot.

Guich hosted a beauty contest during one of those fairs. Anything you thought to be beautiful was to be put on the stage. Entries included babies, dogs and armadillos, and a jar of pickles. No one won the first year.

My husband Dow and I were in charge of the gospel singers on Sunday, who performed off the back of the Pearl Beer flatbed.

LARRY UPSHAW / TEXAS HIGHWAYS

GUICH, THE EMCEE

Also performing on the flatbed, which was the only stage, was local singer-songwriter Rex Foster and some hippie songwriter from Austin named Willie Nelson. The morning after, the grounds looked like a battle scene. Bodies and beer cans lay where they fell. Somewhere under a tree, there'd be a tired worn figure picking out a tune on a guitar waiting for the next go-round.

The '73 Great World's Fair was held before Luckenbach became 75% parking lot. Most of the cars had to park on either side of FM 1376. It was not unusual for persons to have to walk four miles from their parking spot to downtown Luckenbach. So it was decided that the 1974 Fair was to be held at the old fairgrounds in Fredericksburg. Like Luckenbach, it was old and sagging too, but much better suited to large crowds than the open fields of Luckenbach. It had places to sit and restrooms for both sexes.

In 1976, after Hondo died, and Guich Koock left for Hollywood, Guich still continued to stage his favorite event, each year. This time the Great World's Fair of 1977 was held at the new Fredericksburg Fairgrounds.

To promote his sitcom, *Carter Country*, Guich made a deal with ABC-TV to film the fair to promote his show. With such a big crowd in town, the film crew complained that they had to sleep on a motel lawn. John Raven, roving writer for the *Luckenbach Moon*, reported that the parade for the fair was "impressive, a heck of a deal" and can be seen on the website of the Texas Archive of the Moving Image (as "1977 Luckenbach Fair"). Since Fredericksburg's Main Street was made so wide in 1845 to enable the wagons and oxen teams to turn around, the parade could go down one side and come back on the other, seeing both directions at once.

Luckenbach's homespun take on the World's Fair was about chicken flying and armadillo races, which were always the most popular spectator events. Music was non-stop, featuring Marcia Ball on her piano with her band, Freda and the Firedogs. The guy with the motorcycle, Even Steven out of San Antonio, was revving up to get enough distance to qualify for a "Dare-devil Challenge" made between him and big fat Bad McFad (aka John Raven), who was to be shot out of a cannon made of two 50-gallon oil drums; but something failed to work and the challenge fell flat. As with all Great World's Fairs there was something for everyone. Hondo had once written in his *Cedar Creek Clippings*, his take on what a fair would be like:

> *I know lots 'bout huntin', but I don't go much because Mama, my dog, and pet pig always follow. It's kinda like takin' the County Fair with you, Ferris wheel and all.*
>
> – Peter Cedarstacker

(P.S. And yes, we, the Crouch family, really did have a pet pig named Snorton who liked laying in front of our fireplace.)

The last Luckenbach Great World's Fair in 1981 took place on local rancher Roy Petsch's land just down the road from Luckenbach. Grounds were wired for electricity, a concrete dance floor was poured, corrals made for some longhorn cattle and six American Indian teepees were set up. The rattlesnake man Augustine Lopez, again, dumped out a big bag of live rattlesnakes in front of the stage. Folks backed up a respectful 40 feet. He handled them with a snake hook to keep them from crawling off too far. At the conclusion of his demonstration he took them back to his camp to prepare his Texas delicacy, fried rattlesnake.

There were two dozen post-Civil War Cavalry soldiers doing trick riding, picking up a man from the ground, and slashing watermelons with their sabers. A stunt pilot flew over and appeared to crash dive, his engine smoking and sputtering, but pulled out of it at the last minute. What with the Army bugler sounding "Charge!", Indian drums beating, a *mariachi* band playing, it was the last hoorah of the Luckenbach Great World's Fair. Never profitable, but there's always room for doing anything just because it's fun.

Hondo, of little faith, didn't think the 1973 World's Fair would work so he swore he wouldn't come. "To make him mad," Guich said, "we put his picture as a joke on the t-shirt." Of course he came when he heard how many people were there. Plus, we paid off the town note to Benno. It was the only one he attended.

ROBBYN DODD

MUD DOBBER CHILI

The Return of the Mud Daubers to Luckenbach

Luckenbach shuddered under the weight of such huge crowds. The colossal celebrations didn't necessarily make Hondo happy, although he loved being the celebrity of any crowd, reveling with the people. Hondo liked small gatherings. That, and sitting on the bench carrying out the stately business of any other prominent mayor or foreign minister as he interviewed a mud dauber in a cigar box. He declared Luckenbach was the Mud Dauber Capital of the World.

When my parents bought Luckenbach, one of the first things my mother Shatzie did in the store was to take an old box of Post Toasties home to freshen up in the oven. We ate them even though they had a big clay mud dauber nest stuck on the box. There were mud dauber nests on nearly everything in the store.

Just as the swallows return to Capistrano each year and the buzzards return to Hinckley, Ohio... the mud daubers return to Luckenbach. Every return signals the beginning of springtime in the Texas Hill Country. The mud dauber was named the “National Bird of Luckenbach,” although it’s a really a tiny wasp-like insect.

Hondo claimed he could talk to, and understand, mud daubers. He said that Mrs. Mud Dauber once told him that the mud in Grape Creek, which runs through beautiful downtown Luckenbach, was the best mud in the world for building her spring mud nest. Sometimes Hondo’d spray the nests gold and tell the gullible city folks the wasps were getting their dirt from Grape Creek.

I remember his imagineer magic happening when I saw him seemingly talking to himself with a tape recorder and a cigar box. He was actually interviewing a mud dauber caught in the cigar box. He’d occasionally stick the microphone in the box for the wasp’s comment. We preserved this interview on tape.

> ***Hondo***: *I understand this is your national headquarters and that you return here every summer. I would like for you to tell me why all the mud daubers in the world chose Luckenbach as world headquarters. Can you tell me that in a few words?*
>
> ***Mud Dauber***: *Bzzzzzzzzzzzzzzzzzzzzzzzzzzzzzzzzzzzzzzzz.*
>
> ***Hondo***: *I see. You say, uh, once upon a time, a long time ago, about two hundred years you say? A little wounded mud dauber flew into Luckenbach. And that was before white men settled here. And the Indians took this little mud dauber in and kept him until his wing was well. He returned to his little colony of mud daubers and told them about how the friendly the people in Luckenbach were. And, lo and behold, they descended upon Luckenbach the very next summer! Is that right?*

Mud Dauber: *Bzzzzzzzzzzzzzzzzzzzzzzzzzzzzzzzzzzzzzzzzzt.*

Hondo: *Oh thank you. Now, I would like to ask you why you mud daubers have chosen the grocery store-post office-beer joint to build your nests.*

Mud Dauber: *Bzzzzzzzzzzzzzzzzzzzzzzzzzzzzzzzzzzzzzzzzzt.*

Hondo: *I see. Oh, uh, she said that, uh, they picked this spot because they're not bothered. Hee,hee. See, we have no customers here. Uh, very seldom. And, uh, mainly on Sunday, and they don't work on Sunday. Uh, I would also like to ask you, Mr. Mud Dauber, where you're getting your mud now.*

Mud Dauber: *Bzzzzzzzzzzzzzzzzzzzzzzzzzzzzzzzzzzzzzzzzzt.*

Hondo: *Uh, thank you Mr.—uh, oh, I mean, Mrs. Mud Dauber. I forgot. I didn't see your lace panties... Now, could you tell me in just a few short buzzes where you're getting your mud?*

Mud Dauber: *Bzzz, zzzzzzzzz, zzzzzzzzz, zzzz, zzzzzzzzzzzzt.*

Hondo: *Oh, uh, thank you. Folks, this little mud dauber says they get their mud from beautiful downtown Grape Creek in beautiful downtown Luckenbach. It has the best mud daubin' material in the world!*

Hondo's mud dauber wasp interview inspired a yearly celebration, the Return of the Mud Daubers to Luckenbach. And Ray Wylie Hubbard played for years at the dances. "Musically, it's a comfortable place to play. You don't have to worry about your songs going over," he joked. Now Billy Joe Shaver plays for the Dauber Dances. No one was too proud to walk around wearing pipe cleaner mud dauber antennae bobbing from a headband.

Luckenbach and its offbeat celebrations had been a source of comfort and security to Hondo during his lonely last days, following the ending of his 30-year marriage to Shatzie. The people there and their admiration kept him afloat. He received fan mail from as far off as England, Australia, and Canada. In his lifetime, his reward as a character or comic was people's laughter. His cake was his letters. He thrived on the encouragement of strangers. When he went home each night to his quiet, empty house he'd find comfort in reading a letter like this one, from a woman in Los Angeles, California.

> *...Millions of readers from coast to coast got a gift from reading your story... colorful in your western garb, whittling away on Main Street, with apparently nothing to do (for the moment, at least). In reality, you are doing plenty: you're inspiring people. You are a presence, a force...*

The Non-Buy Centennial
1976

In 1976, Luckenbach made national news with its Non-Buy-Centennial Celebration, a protest against the commercialization of America's 200th birthday. Hondo invited the Prince of Wales and Elizabeth Taylor to the shindig.

The unorthodox commemoration was the brainchild of PR man Jack Harmon. Hondo would have preferred to celebrate something simpler, "like the invention of plywood, or the explosion of a gas pump in Pittsburg," he said.

Hondo, from past experience, was concerned about the number of people the event would bring to Luckenbach's fragile ecology. But if Harmon was behind anything, word got around far and wide. And if Hondo was involved, he put forth his natural creativity and became a drawing card by simply being his fun-loving self.

Yellow Dog, the chili cook, organized the world's longest parade a week before to kick off the July 4th event at Luckenbach. The route ran from the Alamo in San Antonio to Luckenbach. I drove Hondo's "float," his truck, in downtown San Antonio, while

NON-BUY CENTENNIAL PARADE, HONDO (PLAYING P-TRAP) AND KATHY MORGAN (WITH BROOM).

AUSTIN AMERICAN-STATESMAN

1976 LUCKENBACH MARCHING BAND

my sons Ren and Kit and friend Bootie waved from the truck bed. The parade took two days to arrive at Luckenbach. Hondo and we didn't follow.

There was much pomp and circumstance as the parade survivors arrived and paraded down or up Luckenbach's Main Street. To start the festivities, the Luckenbach Howitzer was fired. Hondo had spent considerable time collecting a tow sack full of chicken feathers for ammo. The resulting shot leveled the crowd and the feathers, mostly white, gave the feeling of falling snow even though it was the 4th of July.

Hondo marched with Jim Cullum's Happy Jazz Band from San Antonio, playing a sink's p-trap like a trombone (with a kazoo hidden in the mouth of the p-trap).

Wanda Ford, wife of famed Texas architect O'Neil Ford, was in the parade. Wanda was elected the Luckenbach Queen for anything every single year. "We're so conservative," Hondo announced, "we don't throw *anything* away. She'll be our queen every year." Wanda wore a cape and carried a bouquet of peacock feathers that she passed around to admiring children.

Throughout the day "Bad Taste Awards" were announced for the most crass commercialism in the service of our nation's anniversary, such as red, white and blue toilet seats and coffins. The Declaration of Independence was read in its entirety; everyone cheered repeatedly when the phrase "We, therefore, the representatives of the United States of America..." was read.

John Raven, whose role in the festivities was to be shot out of the cannon, remembered everything and told it all well. The big deal of the day was to be the first public appearance of the Big Mother Rocket built by Caliente Chili Rockets and Demolition for Bad McFad (aka John Raven) to ride into glory. The rocket, made of several 55-gallon barrels, painted real nice in different colors, was mounted on top of a 1937 fire truck to make it easier to move.

When the rocket crew—Tom Nall, Charley Fowler, Yeller Dog and Bob Wilson—had all the wires hooked up they took a little break for a cold Big Red.

All the kids in attendance decided the rocket and fire truck were there for climbing on. All the wires were just there to get in their way. You know what happened... When it came time to launch the rocket, Bad McFad climbed aboard and many speeches were made about the wonderful thing that was about to happen. Then came the count-down, "Five, four, three, two, one, BLAST OFF!!" McFad pressed the starter button and nothing happened. The ground crew crawled all over the rocket frantically trying to reconnect the dangling wires.

Finally the crew chief, Charlie Fowler, told McFad to dump the main power supply before something went really bad wrong. McFad tripped the lever and a trap door on the main body of the rocket opened and out fell four or five chickens that had been painted red, white and blue for the holiday. After spending about six hours in the rocket in the hot sun, the chickens were in no condition to fly or do much of anything other than just lay there looking real pitiful and gasping for air. Hondo was heard to say of Bad McFad, "It took a man of that caliber to be loaded into that cannon!"

I didn't attend the event but I heard from friends that Tony Bell fired his Civil War cannon and the masses fell down in the field next to the peach orchard. Hondo awarded purple hearts to those who fell down best. He was jovial and patriotic as he passed around postage stamp-size American flags on toothpicks. "Don't let your flag touch the ground! Wave it high!"

There was a non-flyover by the Navy's Blue Angels. Thousands gazed skywards to view the jets which were not flying over, every hour on the hour. Jim Cullum and his Happy Jazz Band played Dixieland music not far from the General Store on a makeshift stage, while everyone danced everywhere for hours. Under the live oaks, small groups clustered around guitar pickers singing along, clapping, keeping rhythm on homemade jug band instruments. Gallons and gallons of ice-cold beer cooled the dusty-dry throats of participants and spectators alike. The children crawled all over the ancient fire truck, vying for the driver's seat to "p-like" (play like) they were speeding their way to a four-alarm fire.

"Folks around here still believe in America," Hondo said to a reporter. "They're patriotic, conservative, and have a feeling for their caliche soil. But they get a kick out of letting their hair down every now and then, doing something they normally wouldn't find themselves doing."

Hondo let the Luckenbach cult create the zany functions. For example, he refused to participate in their no-talent contest, because, he said, "I have talent." As he'd view the masses roaming the grounds he'd say, "There's no purpose here at all. That's what makes it so great. It's a big nothing and everybody works at it. Look at 'em. I collect funny people. Maybe I'm a kid myself. Maybe I haven't grown up and they all know it. Despite some of the nutty things we do around here, it's still one of the few places I know of where you can stay in touch with reality. Having fun is hard work sometimes."

Once in a while Hondo would attempt to "direct" traffic. Things only got more confused, so he left for a short spell. A total of fifty thousand people attended the Non-Buy-Centennial. Another new record for the record keepers. The only thing Hondo related to me about the celebration was the extraordinary fact that a little frog was pumped out of the hand-pump well where Sam Kindrick was sitting. "The frog jumped right onto the rim of his cup! Sam set him back on the spigot and he jumped right back on the rim of his cup again!" Now *that* was worth remembering!

¡VIVA TERLINGUA!
1973

Things quieted down considerably after the first Great World's Fair. The solitude was short-lived, however, because in '73 Jerry Jeff Walker, one of the most prominent Texan "redneck rock" musicians, recorded his landmark *¡Viva Terlingua!* album live in the dance hall. At the time, it seemed like a lark, but the recording was destined to become one of the most pivotal albums in the history of Texas music.

Scamp Walker *Meets* Scamp Hondo

Luckenbach was becoming established as a shrine for honky-tonk country music. After putting on The Great World's Fair and chili cook-offs, numerous singers and pickers congregated regularly under the trees on Sunday afternoons. If Luckenbach was the shrine, Hondo was the soul. He was an old-time cowboy who embraced grass roots music and celebrated the ceremony of passing the guitar around, sharing the music. No egos found a

TOM WILKES

¡VIVA TERLINGUA! ALBUM COVER

BRYAN HECK

JERRY JEFF WALKER SONG:
"LITTLE BIRD COME SIT UPON MY WINDOW SILL."

pedestal in Luckenbach. Hippie and redneck alike sat side by side on benches, because that was the only place to sit. Music was rich because it was free. At Luckenbach, with Hondo, music was done for the love of the song. It was Hondo's heart and soul that won Jerry Jeff's affection.

In 1965, Jerry Jeff met Hondo through my husband Dow and myself. Ever since, he claimed Hondo as his "old man." "Scamp Walker" was Jerry Jeff's nickname. It took one scamp to recognize another.

It all came about because Dow was double-billed with Jerry Jeff at Austin's Eleventh Door on Red River Street, a folk-genre coffeehouse. Dow saw a skinny guy walking down Red River carrying a guitar case and harmonica rack, and offered him a ride. They happened to be going to the same place.

Crammed together in the little tune-up room behind the stage, Jerry Jeff popped open his guitar case and said, "Listen to this! I just finished writing it. See if you like it!" With his foot on a chair, his Eagle guitar on his lap, with a legal pad and a hard lead pencil, Jerry Jeff said, "I think I've captured this guy." He sang a few verses and then it was time for him to go on. "I'll play it out there. You can hear how it ends."

He sang five verses of "Mr. Bojangles" for the first time, deleting two of the verses by the next night. "It's a true story." he said. "I was in the drunk tank with this white guy in New Orleans. He was a carny, a song-and-dance man, the sort you call a 'bojangles.' He was still grieving over his dog dying."

Dow, being the first pair of ears to hear the future classic, captured it later on his reel-to-reel Wollensak recorder. Later, this song would launch Jerry Jeff into national status when it was recorded by the Nitty Gritty Dirt Band. It became his calling card, a song beloved and recorded by scores of musicians, up to and including Bob Dylan.

Hondo was with us that night. Encouraged by entertainer Allen Damron, and friends in the audience, he eventually ended up on the stage between Allen's, Jerry Jeff's and Dow's acts. "I didn't bring my Mexican union card with me," he blushed as he stole their hearts with "Soy Mexicano del Norte." He was not known by the crowd at that time, but they immediately loved him. Hondo didn't remember meeting Jerry Jeff that night. Hondo was just worried that he couldn't pay the one-dollar cover charge. And he didn't pay.

Jerry Jeff and Hondo met anew one weekend when we took Jerry Jeff out to the ranch. A native New Yorker, the very embodiment of a pale night-owl musician, he showed up wearing rimless milk-of-magnesia blue sunglasses and a blue satin shirt. He'd already changed his real name from Ronald Clyde Crosby to a folkier-sounding name, namely "Jerry Jeff Walker." He devoured three helpings of one of Mama's prize-winning country dinners. "I knew he was a guitar player," Hondo recalled later, "because he was hungry."

Looking back on his time with Hondo, Jerry Jeff related the following tale to me: "I said to Hondo, 'Let's fly up to New York, on me, and you can do your "Daylight" poem with me on stage at Carnegie Hall.' Hondo responded, 'New York! New York'll never amount to anything. It's too far!' He needed to slowpoke it. He liked to stop time.

"One day I was really down, so I called Hondo around 7:30 a.m. 'I'm comin' over,' I told him. So, I sat at his bedside half the morning. He read the paper, drank his Instant Breakfast. I sang to him on his old beat-up guitar. Finally, he bolted outta bed. 'Let's go get some sausage for Luckenbach,' he said, pulling on his blue jeans. 'Come with me.'

"I'm just gonna go wherever you go, Hondo. Want to pick a guitar with you around."

They piled into Jerry Jeff's tan Cadillac. "I'll show you a short cut to Comfort," Hondo confided. The "short cut" was a winding farm-to-market road through the pasture. There they were, two loveable but hard-to-reach renegades, cruising 10 mph down the country road, the Cadillac's sunroof open. Hondo was driving, wearing his black felt Indian hat trimmed with a deer bone hatband. He tugged on a piece of jerky while Jerry Jeff crooned and strummed, his feet propped up on the dashboard. For that moment, time was suspended. Not a care in their minds.

"What do ya think we'd look like if someone met us on the road?" Jerry Jeff was enjoying the scene.

"Don't know. I'd like to own a Cadillac like this." Hondo thought for a moment, then added, "But I'd have to put my chain saw and beer bottles in the back seat."

Jerry Jeff idolized Hondo and his lifestyle at the ranch, to the extent that he bought a place of his own in the Texas Hill Country. On December 12, 1974, Jerry Jeff and Susan Streit exchanged their vows at Luckenbach on the side steps of the bar. It would be the Gillespie County Justice of the Peace Garland Taylor's first of 50 weddings over which he presided at Luckenbach. Garland, tall, rangy and white-haired, remembered, "Jerry Jeff was as nervous as a cat on a hot tin roof." Best Man Hondo wore his tails and top hat for the occasion.

If the Jerry Jeff-Dow Patterson connection hadn't have happened in '65, he wouldn't have met Hondo, and perhaps there'd be no *¡Viva Terlingua!*.

SUSAN AND JERRY JEFF WALKER WEDDING AT LUCKENBACH, 1974.

CENTER: HONDO IN TOP HAT, KATHY MORGAN ON HIS RIGHT, MICHAEL BROVSKY ON HIS LEFT; SUSAN (IN SUNGLASSES) AND JERRY JEFF IN FRONT OF HONDO; BOB LIVINGSTON BELOW JJW (IN HAT);
BACK ROW: ROLAND STOCK (MIDDLE WITH HAT); GARY P. NUNN (HAT, GLASSES) IN FRONT OF ROLAND; JOHN INMON IN FRONT OF GPN, OTHERS: POODIE AND BEAR, BILLIE DON.

LUCKENBACH ARCHIVES

BAFFLING SOUND OF ROOSTERS WITH HAY BALES
FOR RECORDING OF ¡*VIVA TERLINGUA*!

Birth *of* Outlaw Music

"We're all wandering gypsies, Alone"

– by Billy Joe Shaver

Luckenbach is the focal point for me, where everything comes together. It's still this small unpretentious place. But it's big in my mind's eye because of what happened there. Playing Texas music is not necessarily playing country music. It's playing what you feel like playing. That's the spirit of Luckenbach and that's the spirit of Texas.

– Freddy Krc, drummer for Jerry Jeff
and the Gonzo Compadres

The 1970s was the heyday for Texas Outlaw music. The term "outlaw" as it relates to music can be attributed to the Waylon Jennings song, "Ladies Love Outlaws." But it also marked a whole new musical attitude in Texas.

Luckenbach fanned the flame that had already been lit by Waylon Jennings and Willie Nelson and their experiences in the country music industry. Texas songwriters were tired of Nashville's glossy, controlling mentality, so they rebelled, and broke away from Music Row.

"Outlaw," Waylon said, "meant standing up for your own rights, your own way of doing things, and 'outlaw' was as good a description as any." They traded in their "formula" songs for a more poetic, autobiographical, grittier sound. Simpler, honest, with less orchestra. There was a strong emphasis on the Texas tradition of telling stories through music.

Some called this music "cosmic cowboy," after the Michael Martin Murphey song of the same name. Steve Fromholz jokingly called it "The Great Progressive Country Music Scare" of the mid-'70s.

Other genres of music got thrown into the pot. One of Jerry Jeff's band members described it as "rock 'n roll jazz country reggae rhythm and blues Texas roadhouse."

Taking into account their similar songs and lifestyles, some of the main outlaw movement "founders" were Waylon Jennings, Willie Nelson, Jerry Jeff Walker, Billy Joe Shaver, Michael Martin Murphey, Gary P. Nunn, Guy Clark, Townes Van Zandt, Steve Fromholz, Ray Wylie Hubbard, Steve Earle, Butch Hancock, Joe Ely, and Jimmie Dale Gilmore. These and others were the singer-songwriters whom Willie found already playing folk-rock-country-blues in Austin at the Armadillo World Headquarters and other local watering holes in '71 when he arrived to make a fresh, post-Nashville, start.

Austin was a good fit because it had U.T. and was a more liberal town than nearly any other in Texas. It was a good fit for musicians: they had long hair, a laid-back attitude, played to rowdy crowds, and were themselves rowdy and unruly. Jerry Jeff broke the polyester rhinestone dress code with a "who cares" fashion statement. He'd sing his gigs in a bathing suit, boots, vest, T-shirt, bandana, and ball cap.

Luckenbach *Plugged* In

Jerry Jeff recorded three albums in Luckenbach: *¡Viva Terlingua!* (1973), *A Man Must Carry On* (1977), and *Viva Luckenbach* (1994), all recorded wholly or in part in the open dance hall amongst squawking chickens and delirious fans. The location proved his point: he was less interested in the process of *recording* music and more interested in the process of *making* music.

One of the other outlaw ingredients was where the music was recorded. The outlaws started doing that differently, too. Jerry Jeff intensely disliked the coldness of a recording studio, with its over-dubbing and over-perfecting. There were no commercial studios in Austin in that era, so Jerry Jeff rented an old ex-dry cleaners building on Sixth Street where he recorded his *Jerry Jeff Walker* album in 1972. Thus the tradition began. He brought in a portable 16-track machine and the musicians wore bothersome headphones. To ease their jitters, he mixed up a tub of Sangria wine during the sessions, a continuing tradition in itself.

Jerry Jeff had moved to Texas in 1971. "I was burnt-out on touring and doing my singer-songwriter thing across America," he said. "Going to Luckenbach and sitting around the old store, laughing with Hondo and sharing my music with all the locals was what I needed to loosen me up. Hondo would always do his 'Thank you, SIR!!' after I'd pass him, and I'd say, 'Don't call me Sir!', and Hondo would say, 'It don't mean anything, it's just nice to hear.' I'd shake my head and think, 'I've been gone too long.'"

Now that he'd met Hondo—his spiritual mentor—he wanted to record an album out in the cedar breaks. He horrified his bosses at MCA Records by toting his whole Lost Gonzo Band to Luckenbach.

Never mind if Luckenbach wasn't wired for electricity and he forgot to bring any songs.

Jerry Jeff got the idea to record *¡Viva Terlingua!* in Luckenbach when he saw a motorhome plugged into New York City's Town Hall performance space. He hired and brought the very same sound crew, Dale Ashley and Father, to plug their cables into Luckenbach's 1889 dance hall.

It took weeks of preparation, hanging mikes from the trees, cleaning up, banking hay bales everywhere for baffles to muffle roosters crowing. Producer Michael Brovsky, dressed the whole time in his best New York safari suits and platform shoes, helped out by posting this notice for the locals:

> *This tranquil setting will be the location for Jerry Jeff Walker's recording project... It is extremely important that all involved in the project realize that we are trying to capture some of the feeling and magic of the place, we are not trying to take over the town. Rather we will become part of it. All members of the crew, staff and band, will be as unobtrusive as possible, lay back and get into the spirit of it.*

Back in Austin, KOKE-FM's legendary DJ, Joe Gracey, advertised for an audience to come attend a live concert recording. One dollar admission was guaranteed to get a crowd to witness Texas music history in the making. To bait the audience, Jerry Jeff took Hondo with him to KOKE and they sang together on the air.

Jerry Jeff recruited, stole, and branded the musicians he found rehearsing in Austin with Michael Martin Murphey. The *Terlingua* sessions would be the first time they'd play under their new name, "The Lost Gonzo Band." The group was comprised of Gary P. Nunn (piano, vocals); Bob Livingston (bass and vocals); Michael McGeary (drums); Herb Steiner (pedal steel); Craig Hillis (electric guitar); Kelly Dunn (organ and electric piano); Michael Raphael (harmonica). Mary Eagan played fiddle; Joanne Vent sang background vocals.

Jerry Jeff had no idea what to sing, although he wrote five of the nine tracks. Some songs were written right then and there on the spot.

So, he got by with "Gettin' By," typical of his laid-back attitude. The song, the first one on the album, started out, "Hi Buckaroos, Scamp Walker time again!" Jerry Jeff remembered hearing his favorite songwriter Guy Clark's ballad "Desperados Waiting for A Train," so that went into the mix. Ray Wylie Hubbard's "Up Against the Wall, Redneck Mother" was born out of being a hippie trapped in a redneck bar. Jerry Jeff wanted to record it but didn't know the

GONZO COMPADRES; LLOYD MAINES, BOB LIVINGSTON, FREDDY KRC, GARY P. NUNN, JERRY JEFF WALKER, JOHN INMON FOR "VIVA LUCKENBACH" ALBUM, 1993.

third verse. Bob Livingston found a pay phone, called Ray Wylie, and Hubbard wrote the third verse while on the phone. The chorus would've been enough.

Jerry Jeff's musical influences were Babe Stovall (a New Orleans street musician), Ramblin' Jack Elliott and Django Reinhardt. You can hear it in his songs. Jerry Jeff could always bump the tempo of a slow melancholy song into a more upbeat "romp." He sang Michael Martin Murphey's "Backslider's Wine" more as a folk-gospel treatment instead of Murphy's gospel-folk. Gary P. recalled the fun he had singing harmony with Hondo on "Sangria Wine." Afterwards, Hondo's voice could be heard on tape correcting, "No, it's *Sangrita* wine!"

The music didn't stop when the tapes stopped rolling. Gary P. Nunn recalled, "I can remember often we would gather outside the post office/beer joint after the session, and continue to pick and pass songs along. One evening the chickens and the guineas were going to roost in the trees above, cackling and squawking. It reminded me of the pick-a-little-talk-a-little version of "Goodnight

Ladies" from the musical, *The Music Man*. Bob Livingston and I broke into the tune. It eventually ended up on the *!Viva Terlingua!* LP. Usually Jerry Jeff would prevail on Hondo to recite his 'Luckenbach Moon' poem, or sometimes, if we stayed up all night, he would do 'Luckenbach Daylight.' More magic."

The stage and hay bales took up half the dance floor. People were sitting in windows, hundreds inside and outside. My friend, Tom Nall (of Two-Alarm and Republic Tequila fame) and brother Blue, just blew in from Dallas that weekend, unaware of anything going on. They saw Brovsky's ad on the door and the $1.00 admission fee. They stayed all week, camping across the creek in their cowboy teepee. Gary P. Nunn was camped there also, in a real Indian teepee.

"All the rehearsing was going on in the bar and the female singer from Florida was practicing singing her little heart out, putting her soul into it," Tom Nall remembered. Meanwhile, his brother Blue fell out of the dance hall window and landed at the feet of an old couple. "Well, I got bucked off again," he told them.

Blue ended up sitting on the curb, so as to have not so far to fall, along with the photographer Tom Wilkes, who did the *¡Viva Terlingua!* album cover design and photo. Tom also had designed the Rolling Stones' lips logo. The cover photo was of the bar door, which just happened to have the Terlingua (chili cook-off site) bumper sticker on it. Hondo's finger pointed to the $1.00 cover charge.

On Saturday the 18th, a huge enthusiastic crowd turned out due to two days of Austin's KOKE Radio blitz. The place was packed with people hanging out of the windows and literally from the rafters.

Impromptu, on stage that night, Jerry Jeff told Gary, "Sing that song you were playing this afternoon, the one from London!" Gary P. Nunn's "London Homesick Blues" was written when he went across the Pond to help Michael Martin Murphey promote the

Cosmic Cowboy Souvenir album in England. He slept in Murphy's brother-in-law's flat. And yes, like the song said, "Well, it was cold over there, and I swear, I wish they'd turn the heat on."

The *¡Viva Terlingua!* concert was the first time that tune had ever been performed onstage. Although the Gonzos had never played it, they soon caught on and the band and crowd went wild singing the now-famous chorus that most Texans know by heart:

> *I want to go home with the armadillo,*
> *Good country music from Amarillo and Abilene,*
> *The friendliest people and the prettiest women you've ever seen.*
>
> *... And of the whole damn lot,*
> *The only friend I've got,*
> *Is a smoke and a cheap guitar.*
> *My mind keeps roamin',*
> *My heart keeps longin',*
> *To be home in the Luckenbach bar.*

If you ask Gary P. if "armadillo" meant the animal or the place, Armadillo World Headquarters, he'd say, "armadillo" referred to the hippie back-to-the-land people of the '70s. The quintessential song made its debut that night at Luckenbach. "It was the highlight of my entire career," said Gary P. "The rest is history."

Of the "Five Essential Albums" (cited in the April 2012 issue of *Texas Monthly* magazine), Jerry Jeff Walker's *¡Viva Terlingua!* was arguably the most consequential. It did then, and still does, embody the rambunctious, freewheeling spirit of musical discovery that embodied the era. Of the "Ten Essential Songs" mentioned in the same issue, most are connected to Luckenbach as well:

> *Guy Clark's "L.A. Freeway," Waylon's "Luckenbach, Texas (Back To the Basics of Love)," Willie's "Blue Eyes Cryin' In the Rain" and Jerry Jeff's "Hill Country Rain."*
>
> *(Jerry Jeff actually mentioned me in his album's liner notes as inspiration for "Hill Country Rain." As we were getting drenched from a sudden downpour at Johnson City's July Fourth, I mentioned how we little Crouch kids would run around naked in the rain.)*

Murphey himself said his *Cosmic Cowboy Souvenir* album was the first to directly address what was happening in the Austin music scene. But of Jerry Jeff, who stole away his musicians, Murphey said that the *¡Viva Terlingua!* album wiped out everything else.

Steve Earle summed it up when he said that, "The thing that has lasted from that time was the music. It really was a special time. That's why people are still talking about it."

John Inmon, who was the Gonzos' lead guitarist for many years said, "Simply, Jerry Jeff made recording fun!"

You Don't Know What You Got Til You Got Nunn

The making of the *¡Viva Terlingua!* album was an undertaking that showcased some of Texas' most talented songwriters: Gary P. Nunn, Jerry Jeff, Guy Clark and Ray Wylie Hubbard, were among the "picker poets" who would be bound together artistically and emotionally after the *Terlingua* sessions, swapping songs and picking on each others' albums. If Waylon sang about getting back to the basics of life, Gary P. nailed a homegrown *joi de vie* about Texas with "Road Trip", about Highway 281, the curving scenic road that runs north and south through the heart of the Hill Country.

We're goin' cruising down 281
We'll be two-steppin', skinny dippin, soakin' up the sun
With the top down, getting brown
Ain't it good to be alive!
We'll sing a chili song—there's a party comin' on.
We're gonna cut some rug til the cows come home.
Lookin' like a Luckenbach good time Saturday night.

HONDO AND YOUNG GARY P.

Gary P. Nunn, one of Texas' best ambassadors and troubadours, sings about what we all love and feel about the culture of fun in Texas.

"London Homesick Blues" sold over a million copies on *¡Viva Terlingua!* and was the theme song for 28 years on the famed *Austin City Limits* TV show. *Texas Music* magazine said the quintessential Texas experience would be to dance to that song at Luckenbach.

Gary P. has been a tradition at Luckenbach since 1973. His sincerity, genuine sense of fun, and laid-back demeanor makes you feel like he personally wants you to have a good time.

The Luckenbach connection, he reminded me, went back to 1973 when he met Hondo in Austin at Tim O'Connor's bar, Castle Creek. Gary P. and John Inmon had just split up with Michael Murphey and joined up with Jerry Jeff's band, which had changed its name from the Deaf Cowboy Band to the Lost Gonzo Band.

He was 28, and on their first meeting Hondo asked him why he didn't cut his hair and beard. When Gary P. arrived in Luckenbach to help Jerry Jeff record *¡Viva Terlingua!* album he had cut his hair and beard just for Hondo.

"Just meeting and getting to know this magical man is one of the highlights of my life," Gary explained. "He was totally enchanting, and I, like so many others he touched, fell under his spell. He made me feel very special. He influenced me the rest of my life. He always was way ahead of you, always planning, in an intuitive way."

Gary P. wanted to name his newborn son "Lucken Bach Nunn." His wife settled for "Lucken," spelled "Lukin" at that. During the recording of Walker's second record album at Luckenbach in '76 (*A Man Must Carry On*), Gary P. and his wife Karen stayed the whole time in a real Indian teepee on the creek bank.

After the recording session finished and everyone had gone, Hondo called the store to get someone to tell Gary P., "Don't let him leave 'til I get back." He came back with a gift for toddler Lukin, a train engineer's striped overalls with matching cap, complete with a red bandana. He would usually include in a gift like that the contents of a little boy's pockets: already chewed chewing gum, a wad of tin foil, string, a broken arrowhead, a matchbox containing a real live fuzzy caterpillar.

Years later, Gary P. gave Hondo the guitar on which he had written "London Homesick Blues." It was a simple classical guitar like Hondo played. "I gave him my guitar," Gary P. said. "But Jerry Jeff said he gave him his heart."

"Two weeks after the recording of A Man Must Carry On, on September 27," Gary P. recalled, "Hondo died; from all the sleepless story-telling jamming nights under the oak trees, we'd feared. The album then took on a different mood and purpose. Relationships are born here but they never die here." We "*chew on the good times and spit out the bad*", as Gary P sings. When *A Man Must Carry On* was released the next year, it had been re-fashioned as a tribute to Hondo.

Since then, we've danced a lot of miles with Gary P., whether it be a sweet waltz or a sweaty swing. Whenever I hear the sparkle in his voice, brought forth by that famous smile, I breathe deep and feel at home listening to him. He sings about cook-offs, Terlingua skies and the Guadalupe River. We float and twirl with him, unified by that same big blue sky canopy that stretches from down in the Big Bend all the way up to the Hill Country that covers us all. His "Ask Me What I Like About Texas" is a classic portrait describing our varied regions as well as characters. Gary P. never takes himself too seriously.

Born in Okmulgee, Oklahoma, Gary P. lived with his second wife, Ruth, on family land in Oklahoma. When his 30-year-old horse died he moved to Texas permanently. He built a house near Marble Falls. "My favorite kind of tour," he said, "would be playing in those old dance halls with open windows, like Gruene Hall, the Broken Spoke, and Luckenbach."

He worked on a live album. He wanted to put classic honky-tonk songs on it like Red Steagall's "Lone Star Beer and Bob Wills Music" and "A Heart Shaped Like Texas." He sees himself as keeping up the traditions as Bob Wills, the Texas Playboys, Hank Thompson, Ray Price, and Ernest Tubb, playing the honky-tonks and dance halls.

"I like dances where the whole family can come and the kids can run around," he said. I told him that's the way my parents raised us. Mama and Hondo, expert dancers, square-danced and did Mexican folk dancing. People would stop and stare at them doing the polka. Many a night we kids slept under the tables on the *rode decca* (red blanket) at such open air dance halls as Crider's in the tiny Hill Country town of Hunt.

Gary P. is a craftsman of a songwriter. I like the hooks in his lines. One catchy hook on one of Gary P.'s songs was recorded by Willie: "The last thing I needed the first thing this morning was to have you walk out on me."

I like the title of, "Don't Get Me Started If You Don't Want to Go All the Way." I told him to write a song to go with a title my husband Dow Patterson thought up: "I Always Hit the Ceiling When You Drive Me Up the Wall." We all still think Susanna Clark, Guy's wife, had the best title: "If You Don't Leave Me Alone, I'll Find Someone Who Will."

Gary P. Nunn has returned to Luckenbach faithfully for 44 years for the Cowboy Christmas Ball and the "Hug-In" Valentine's dance.

In October 2017, he came back to Luckenbach to do a fundraiser for victims of Hurricane Harvey, the storm that had inflicted such terrible damage on the Texas coast. As usual, it was a "fun" raiser. Days later, I'm still thinking about and basking in the feelings of that Sunday afternoon with Gary P. Hard to believe something that good is also that lasting.

Throughout all these years he has become legendary in Texas music as a writer and performer, but he has never gotten too big for us. Here at Luckenbach we may have a little dance hall, but we have a big moon, and we also have Gary P. with his big heart. They made a state park out of the Big Blanco River. But we here at Luckenbach are like the Little Blanco River, still running but not big enough to be a state park. Like the Little Blanco River, Gary P., don't ever get too big for us. Please keep runnin' and comin'. Like you sing in the songs,

We don't know what we got when we got it.
We don't know what we're missing til we've tried it.

"Terlingua Sky"
by Larry Joe Taylor

We've come a long long way
And we've got a long way to go.

"A Long Way to Go"
by Davin James

ROBBYN DODD

GARY P. NUNN'S LONGHORN BOOTS

"I'M *Not* HERE ANYMORE"

"I'm not here anymore—H," read the cryptic note we found at our back door after one of Hondo's visits to our house in San Antonio. In typical Hondo fashion, it left one feeling not only the *absence* of a presence, but the *presence* of the spirit of the now-absent visitor. It was Valentine's Day and the boys were eager to see what he'd left each of them in two little brown paper sacks; not candy, but a can of sardines and crackers. He always shook up our expectations; left us wanting more.

Last Sightings *of* Hondo

The older Hondo got, the more beautiful he became. His appearance anywhere was a show-stopper. And his charming (though contrived) innocence dominated everything he did. I can see him now as he walked through the doors of a prestigious hotel in Las Vegas with his friend Madge Reid. The lobby was filled with persons attired in flashy apparel, their concentration entirely upon the slot machines before them.

ALLEN DAMRON AND HONDO AT KERRVILLE FOLK FESTIVAL
PERFORMING "LUCKENBACH DAYLIGHT"

Madge recalled, "I believe Jesus could have walked down the corridor and not one head would have lifted!" But as Hondo entered, dressed in his usual faded denims, stuffed into his knee-high boots, heads turned. Slot machines ceased their noise. "Everyone was looking at us. It was Hondo. He was just plain beautiful to behold in his beat up ol' cowboy hat. They recognized a genuine cowboy from a drugstore one."

Even after Hondo was gone, I kept expecting him to appear magically from nowhere as he always seemed to do while he lived. He had a way of coming into a room quietly and standing there until he got noticed. Seeing him, you couldn't help but smile.

Under the dazzling glow of the ceiling light at ritzy Houston's ritzy River Oaks Country Club, his white hair gleamed like an angel's. He was attending a debutante party with his friend Gloria Hill. As he stood there in his rented Prince Edward-style tux, a stranger approached him. "Sir, I don't know who you are but my wife thinks you are the prettiest thing she's ever seen in her life. Would you please come meet her?"

One of the last unexpected things I did with Hondo was to accompany him in the parade in San Antonio, which I've mentioned before, the one organized to advertise his Non-Buy-Centennial at Luckenbach, a protest against the commercialization of the nation's 1976 Bicentennial. Hondo rang our doorbell. A friend of mine answered the door to find Hondo standing there with a "Sanitized for Your Protection" toilet band across the front of his blue jeaned lap. "This must be Hondo," she called to me from the door.

He was inviting us to ride with him in the "World's Longest Parade," from the Alamo to Luckenbach. I saw a rough pine casket in the back of his truck. It had been awarded him by the director of the recent film, *Pony Express Rider*, in which he'd appeared. He just never took it out of his truck; kept it in order to "be prepared to go at any time." Eyeing the coffin and imagining the other characters that would be accompanying him, I was hesitant.

"Oh, come on! Let's go!" urged my friend Bootie. Bootie sat atop the casket waving to the cheering crowd like a parade queen, and my boys were her T-shirted attendants. I drove the truck while Hondo, in an armadillo helmet, led his unusual assortment of pick-up truck "floats" down Broadway. The seventy-mile parade took two days to reach Luckenbach. It rained the whole way, but nothing could dampen peoples' spirits while they were with Hondo.

Hondo was a tragic Shakespearean hero like King Lear, who seemingly had everything but happiness. He never got over losing his son to mental illness. Kerry, a math genius, who'd been accepted at MIT, was a straight-A student of architecture at U.T. At age eighteen, he'd already built his own creative house in Austin. Under the pressures of school, two jobs, worry about his brother Juan in Viet Nam, Kerry tragically disappeared into schizophrenia at twenty-one. Hondo would never know that Kerry would eventually take his own life. It had been four years after Hondo and Shatzie's divorce that had left him totally depressed.

Now it was a miracle, we thought, that he was finally pulling out of it, repaying the world with gratitude, not bitterness. At home, alone, Hondo grew increasingly more thankful for simple things. He told me, "I was just laying in my bed the other morning and I thanked God for all he's done for me. I have a nice warm house, a truck, and bed, and toothpaste. Imagine that! Not everyone has toothpaste!" As our family gathered on Christmas Eve, he recited his new poem, "Luckenbach Daylight," just to us, at Cris' house. It would be recorded live at the next Kerrville Folk Festival, where he was one of their icons, to the accompaniment of softly played guitar music.

Luckenbach Daylight

Nuthin' much happened in Luckenbach this month... 'cept the potato chip man came by—I forgot about that—and then there was Daylight!

A Luckenbach daylight is the time of day you wish would never go away... when BANG!... all of a sudden there's no dark and there's no light, and it's foggy—and it isn't! It's as humble as life being born! Ain't that nearly a blessin'?!

Daylight on earth is when light is busy makin' little ol' nothins onto somethins... and sometimes big brown bears turn into just big brown rocks.

Daylight in the wintertime is when little drippin' icicles get a new hold on their host... and Jack Frost is busy rolling up his carpet (Always from East to West) that covers the hills we love so.

Daylight in Spring is when little ol' ladies are thinkin' 'bout puttin' on big ol' bonnets and long sleeves to hide from the sun... and little young ladies are thinkin' about takin' off their clothes to lie in it!—Scare me!

And Mama's thinking about pullin' the shades in the livin' room—where nobody has ever really lived—so the sun won't sad the colors of the rug.

Daylight in the Fall is when big-eyed deer get closer to the ground—cause they know red-eyed hunters with heavy rifles will soon be stumblin' through the brush again-and-again-and again.

And big trees brace themselves. The first norther's gonna tug pretty colors out of just plain leaves... and then walk off.

A Luckenbach daylight is that magic time of day when there's just thousands of insignificant miracles happenin'. Little quiet night feet are softly remembering their way home... And soon their little delicate night tracks will be erased by big fussy day ones.

And the squawkin' mockin' bird will wake the sun. And the sun will tell the mama hoot owl it's time to fuss her big-eyed babies to bed...

And all the stars that were admired last night will take a back seat in the bus... And the fantastic firefly will be just a bug. But a giant weed will turn into a beautiful sunflower!

Then there's that unbelievable... unbelievable smell of fresh coffee!... and leathery ranchers sittin' around sippin' too many cups... just to keep from going to work—until the distant, insistent naggin' of a chain saw jerks 'em back to reality.

Little empty lunch pails are meetin' full ones on the freeway.

You know—my music-makin' friends never get to enjoy all this... they're too busy racin' the day home.

Sad folks wake up and say, "Nuther day." I wake up and say, "There she is again! There it is!" Isn't that funny... all this pretty stuff doesn't happen unless I'm there.

I get on my knees and pat the earth and say, "God, you done good! Thank you, feller... friend!"

Jerry Jeff told me, "I wanted to be more like Hondo. I needed a little more of his goodness and he needed a little more of my badness. He was always tryin' to get me to say, 'Thank you, friend!' to God. But even if I ever do—I'll always have the blues."

"My favorite times," Jerry Jeff said, "were after we closed the store and drove the back road over to Hondo's ranch. We would sit out on the back patio under the stars, drink beer, eat jerky, tell stories, and sing songs til the sun came up. That's when Hondo recited the 'Luckenbach Daylight' poem, as the sun was coming up. When I heard him recite his 'Daylight' poem on the patio at his ranch, that line that said, 'None of this pretty stuff happens 'less I'm there,' I jumped up and hugged him. It was daylight on the patio. That's the way I'll always see him."

Hondo had written two poetic narrations prior to his death, "Luckenbach Moon" and "Luckenbach Daylight." He was working on a third when he died. It remains unfinished:

Luckenbach Sundown

I can watch the sun going down from the patio.
It's the only time of day you can see it from here.
There's barefooted porchy folks catchin' up on their sittin',
Too tired to rock against the grain,
So they rock with it.
I can see the smoke from the little kitchen windows following
the sun to the horizon.
And there it is...
Just sitting.
Pooching its cheeks out,
Holding its breath,
Trying not to leave this pretty world I
live in...

The last time I saw Hondo, I had taken him to the fancy Bright Shawl Tea Room in San Antonio to have brunch. It was my sister Cris's first day to wait tables there. She was so nervous she poured ice water into Hondo's coffee cup. Hondo tipped her a penny. When he paid the check at the cash register I remember him tearing brand new bills from a tablet of tens. 'That new money smells funny," I commented. I'd never seen a *tablet* of money before.

"That's cause I keep it in my sock," he said, embarrassing the cashier. "All the money that I make underneath the house smells funny anyway."

We drove him to the parking lot where his truck was parked. He went to it and brought me a gift from the cab. "I've been saving these for you. Make something pretty out of them." He handed me the tips of two white cow tails. Then, handing me an old rusted belt buckle, he said, "I was going to put this on a belt, but I could see it as a necklace on you." Then he handed me a smooth river rock. "When you hold this in your hand," he said, "remember, wherever you are, you're in the center of the universe." I took the gifts. We didn't say goodbye. It always hurt a little. He drove off and I returned home casually thinking I'd see him again tomorrow. I never saw him again.

The *A Man Must Carry On* album that Jerry Jeff had started recording at Luckenbach ended up including Hondo reciting the "Luckenbach Moon" poem and three of Charles John Quarto's poems honoring Hondo. Quarto stayed with us at the ranch for days at a time, writing those poignant poems.

The Luckenbach Moon

Nuthin' much happened in Luckenbach this month,
'Cept the potato chip man came by.
Then there was the moon.
We try to tell folks who come by here to look at our town
What a big, mean moon we have
But nobody'll believe it.
And last night it showed off.
The greatest ever.
It just hung there, darin' you to look at it,
Makin' silhouettes into things and things came alive.
It even shined plumb to the bottom of the canyon,

Under bluffs and plopped dark doughnuts 'round the bottom of trees on top of the mountain.
A kind of moon that makes haunted houses uglier
And ugly girls prettier.
And little animals see farther and feel closer together.
Brave weeds even rose up to look 'round for lawn mowers.
Grandpa sat up in bed and said, "What's that?"
And the hair on Grandpa's legs stood on end, he said.
On moonbright night like this, big eyed deer
Tiptoe into larger openings and they can dance better 'cause they can see where the rocks are at.
Their prancin' gets fancier and freer because they know mans Not there to dampen the dance.
This kind of moonshine makes you crazy if you sleep in it,
they say.
But I think you're crazy not to try it.
Momma even slept with the baby to protect it and I
Flounced in bed even in a thick rock house.
And when I went outside to see what was the matter
Somethin' scared cold chills up my back.
Everything was standin' at attention over new shadows.
Then what was that that moved?
Probably just a nuthin'.
You know, a big full moon like ours is kinda like a person:
It needs help to show off, and last nite
All the clouds stayed home on purpose
To create a great solo.
We can't stand an encore!
It takes too much out of you.
Those who saw the moon said they could smell it.
One said it tasted like sin.
The quietness at the parkside road was deafenin'
And the little single couple sittin' there touched
The backs of their hands together.
"Scare Me!"
We've been tellin' strangers who come to Luckenbach
'Bout our Moon,
But I know they won't believe that
We have such a big moon
For such a small town.

Willie Nelson remembered Hondo from the several times he came to Luckenbach. "Hondo Crouch wasn't just a funny, friendly guy. He was a poet, and a good one. His poetry came hard, like all good poems do—like the crops in the Hill Country that somehow grow in spite of the cold, the hot sun and the rocks.

"Hondo carried a little notebook with him and he'd finally find that stubby pencil in his pocket somewhere. Then he'd write down his poems and whittle at the words with the same skill and insistence that marked his wood carvings. Like everybody else, I loved Hondo and remember him under the trees reciting 'Luckenbach Moon.' I wish everyone could have heard him do that before he died. We still have him doing it on the great record, but the record can't give us back the twinkle and the grin—the whole being that shined like a Hill Country stream on a sunny spring day. You should have seen Hondo when he did 'Luckenbach Moon.' I was lucky. I did."

His Heart Was So Full Of Mischief
by Charles John Quarto

Texas swing out of your saddles
Abilene pick up your cards
Houston blink up from your blueprints
Dallas stop smiling so hard
One of your cowboys is missing
By the name of Hondo Crouch
His heart was so full of mischief
It grinned open and slipped out.
From raising sheep and eyebrows
To singing asleep with beer
He was the Sunday Mayor of Luckenbach
And the grand imagineer
He held conversations looking sideways
Tugging his mustache toy
His remarks always seemed like secrets
Kept between gray haired boys
Heck, he was a talking treasure
Though his tongue stayed in his cheek
He spread a blanket of stories over Texas
So other storytellers could sleep.

Jerry Jeff Sightings

During his pilgrimage to the Terlingua Chili Cook-Off, Hondo's admirers flocked around him, whether they knew who he was or not. Kirk Dooley, a writer for the U.T. student newspaper, the *Daily Texan*, was introduced to Hondo thusly:

> *Kirk said, "A group of us led the crowd to believe Jerry Jeff Walker was with us. A friend who looked like Walker stumbled out of our motor home and the crowd went wild. We fooled them all. Cameras clicked. Autograph hounds swooped in. When the crowd was finally gone, a little old man—a cute little old man—walked up with head bowed and asked if he could say hello to Jerry Jeff. We said sure.*
>
> *"Head bowed like he was addressing a king, he said, 'Mr. Walker. It sure is a pleasure to make your acquaintance, sir. You're one of my favorite singers and I just wanted to tell you that. I'm sorry that I took up some of your time.' He looked up for a second then humbly walked away.*
>
> *"We felt terrible. There was a knot in my stomach. We had taken advantage of a poor old man and we quickly agreed to call off our little joke. I went after the old man but there was a crowd of people around him. I asked if anyone knew the guy's name and two people turned around and said, 'Sure, he's Hondo Crouch, Jerry Jeff Walker's best friend. Everybody knows Hondo!'"*

Jerry Jeff once said of Hondo, "He reminded me of a magician friend in New York—when he wanted to show me how the trick worked, I'd say 'No! Don't!' I always want to be fooled."

"One time," Jerry Jeff recalled, "I asked Hondo if he believed in reincarnation what would he come back as. 'A little poodle,' he answered, 'carried around on a pillow so someone would pet me, and brush my hair.' No, Hondo! Wouldn't you rather be a sheepdog? Hondo answered, 'No. I was already that in this life!' "

GARY P. NUNN

HONDO'S ROPE TRICK.
1973

Hondo once told me, "They're gonna write 'He never made it' on my tombstone someday. He also said, "People think they know me but no one ever will." Naomi Shihab Nye wrote a haunting song about that comment. When Dow Patterson and I sang it at one of Lady Bird Johnson's private dinner parties, one of President Johnson's speech writers, intrigued by it, came up to us and asked us for the words. Here they are:

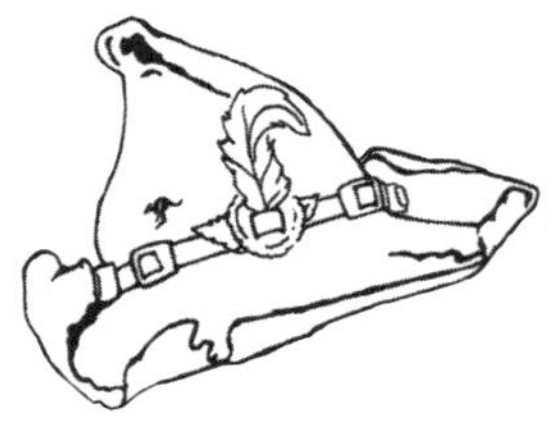

Hondo's Lament

by Naomi Shihab Nye
and John Paul Walters

I am the name that you know and yet nobody knew me
I am the place where you go when you go there alone
Where are these hills that I lived in and loved in for so long?
... And where is the song that always reminds me of home?

I am the prairie that no one will ever discover.
I am the lover of miracles small to behold.
Arrowheads shaped by the hands of the ones who once lived here
And quiet compadre of anything humble and old.

(guitar/fiddle interlude)

Bridge:
Everyone told me I was a tree they could lean on
Everyone shook me to see if my branches were real
They didn't know that I wasn't the hero they needed
That I was a man who was lonely, like something you dream of forever but never quite feel...

Find an old trail that goes nowhere you ever remember,
Find an old river that never will tell of your tears
Just like a snake who can lose its old skin and continue
Climbing back out of a canyon he filled with his years.

(guitar/fiddle interlude)
(Repeat verse one:..."and where is the song that always reminds me of home?")

"A Man *Must* Carry On"

Jerry Jeff was recording his latest album at Luckenbach at the time of Hondo's death in 1976. Therefore, he decided to name it "A Man Must Carry On." It became a beautiful tribute to him.

Right before the end, Hondo had stayed up all night, several nights in succession, with the enduring drinkers and pickers. The marathon jam session took its toll. On September 27th, Kathy Morgan, Hondo's Luckenbach partner, called Jerry Jeff to say Hondo had died of a heart attack. She heard him drop the phone and he never returned to pick it up. Jerry Jeff's love affair with Hondo from 1965–'76 was too short-lived.

Willie Nelson sat quietly unnoticed out in his van at the funeral at St. Barnabas Episcopal Church in Fredericksburg, along with hundreds of others in the overflow crowd. In a pasture that the local hunters named Camp-Wait-A-Minute, we put Hondo's ashes in an armadillo hole at the Laughing Tree. Hondo gave the tree that name because it had a big burl that looked like a beehive in the B'rer Rabbit stories. Cows surrounded us with a mournful chorus of mooing and bellowing, thinking they were going to be fed.

SceneMagazine
THE DALLAS MORNING NEWS
FEBRUARY 18, 1979

Requiem for a Clown Prince

. . . plus a special **HomeScene** section on lawns and gardens

REQUIEM FOR A CLOWN PRINCE, 1976.
SCENE MAGAZINE, DALLAS MORNING NEWS

"LET'S GO *to* LUCKENBACH TEXAS BACK *to the* BASICS"

1977

– sung by Waylon and Willie and the Boys

"Well, wouldn't ya just know it? Just about the time this tiny little town gets back to being sleepy *again*, here they come with that song!" said Luckenbach native and bartender Sheriff Marge Ottmers Mueller. "The first time I heard it was when someone played it for me over the phone! I said, 'You're kidding!' I can't wait to hear it again!" Hondo's former partner Guich Koock, who was then living and working in Hollywood, ran into Willie Nelson at The Troubadour. He told Guich, "We just recorded a song called 'Luckenbach, Texas,' and it's gonna be Number One."

"Luckenbach's really going to change," predicted Guich. "I like it the way it is."

Guy Clark was the catalyst for the creation of the song, and Hondo was the inspiration. Guy, one of Jerry Jeff's favorite writers, penned "Desperados Waiting For A Train," which Jerry Jeff included on the *¡Viva Terlingua!* album. As he was an old friend of our

THE RECORD SIGNED TO ME BY CHIPS MOMAN AND BOBBY EMMONS

RICHARD PRUITT

1960, WHEN I MET GUY CLARK

family from years ago, we kept up with Guy, especially when he did gigs around the Texas Hill Country. Guy visited Luckenbach after Hondo died in '76. Every concert and music festival in Texas at the time was being dedicated to Hondo.

Guy and his wife Susanna returned home to Nashville, telling veteran songwriter Bobby Emmons and Bobby's partner/producer Chips Moman about the quaintness of Luckenbach.

"Y'all oughta go there sometime!" encouraged Guy. Bobby Emmons, who cut his teeth on R & B at Memphis' famed American Studio, in return replied, "Why don't you write a song about it, Guy?" To which Guy replied, "Why don't *you*?!" The rest is history.

Although neither Chips nor Bobby ever visited Luckenbach, Emmons said, "We had already been talking about this 'basics' idea for a song, and the two concepts got together some way. I had been talking about 'back to the basics' and Chips and I were talking about putting on jeans and let everything drop."

The song became Number One for weeks on both the country and popular music charts, and ended up as one of the biggest hits of 1977. Even so, many stations in the Texas portion of the Bible Belt wouldn't play the song. They objected to the first line and its reference to "firm-feelin' women." If you called up Luckenbach on its only phone, you'd hear a menu on the answering machine with Waylon singing the first line.

Though Luckenbach already had a large and loyal cult following, it now additionally had to deal with mega-popularity and a whole new swarm of curious visitors. Some of them were eager to have their own little piece of Luckenbach, so they took it. Boards from the cotton gin, signs off the buildings, pictures in the store, the one parking meter and even Hondo's revered guitar fell victim to souvenir seekers.

Zip Zimmerman, the town's security guard, remembers the change the song made. "Three to four thousand tourists came to

Luckenbach daily. They took souvenirs—longnecks, rocks, signs, anything, eventually the old fire truck—till the place was picked clean by the buzzards.

"You never knew who was going to show up," Zip said. "One day a balding man wearing a squash blossom necklace walked in. I knew he was the son of the movie star Peter Lorre because he looked and sounded exactly like his dad. The locals would sit together at the table in front of the dance hall just to watch the tourists. It was their favorite pastime. They were amazed." For his part, Guich remembered one time Ansel Adams, the most important landscape photographer of the 20th Century, came to Luckenbach and went around taking photographs.

No highway signs pointed the direction to Luckenbach because they'd been swiped, too. "Maybe it's a blessing," co-owner Kathy Morgan sighed. "At least this way, only the people who really want to come will find us."

The song brought national attention, and a lot of tour buses to Luckenbach the year after Hondo died. That kind of publicity and the thousands of people it brought had always made Hondo doubtful as Luckenbach attracted more notice when he was alive. Publicizing Luckenbach wasn't what Hondo had in mind. Chips Moman recalled how Hondo had described it: "Luckenbach is my antique rocking chair. Come sit in it with me, but don't molest my rockin' chair."

Guy Clark

Guy Clark was a true poet. His ideas for songs always turned out winners, were soulful, and were usually stories about Texas.

GUY CLARK'S LAST APPEARANCE AT LUCKENBACH, 2008

My early years of knowing him began in 1960. Guy was 20 and I was 16. I had a crush on him and those deep-set eyes that lasted the rest of my life.

In 1960, it was there in his hometown of Rockport, on the Texas Gulf Coast, that I experienced one of the first of many picker circles at my *Tia's* (my aunt, Hondo's sister) beachfront cottage. Hondo and his longtime friends, Gloria and George Hill, a lawyer from Houston, sang as a trio—Sons of the Pioneers songs and Mexican songs, better than the Mexicans. Also in the circle was Lola Bonner, law partner of Guy's dad Ellis, who sang and played beautifully with her guitar. (Guy would one day immortalize his father in his masterful song, "The Randall Knife.")

Guy wasn't a songwriter yet, but went on to Houston to make and repair guitars. "I'll never forget Hondo singing those Mexican songs," he told me. "So, the closest I could come to that was to work on *Spanish* guitars." The last time Guy came to Luckenbach was in 2008 to sing in Mike Blakeley's Fandango, a showcase of songwriters, authors and artists.

In May, 2016, the last idea Guy had for a song was right before he died. Running out of energy, he called up fellow Houstonian and songwriting collaborator, Rodney Crowell. He told Rodney about seeing a crow's nest in a windmill made out of barbed wire. The image conjured up a physical symbol of what my mother Shatzie always said, "I'm comfortable being uncomfortable." Rodney finished the song Guy started. Old songwriters never die. Their songs just keep on breathing. He was the songwriter's songwriter; one of the best.

In tribute, Rodney Crowell wrote a song to his friend Guy, about their admiration and friendship, one poet to another.

May the wind be at your back
And the world sit at your feet
May you waltz across Wyoming

With a rose clenched in your teeth
May the answers to your questions
Fall like raindrops right on cue
May you set up shop in Heaven
'Fore the Devil knows you're due
Here's to me
Here's to you
Some ol' mad dog mountain flyboy
And the kid from Tennessee

"The Flyboy and the Kid"
by Rodney Crowell

Guy Clark died in 2016. He was 74. Before he died, Guy had also talked to his friend, artist/sculptor/singer Terry Allen, about one last request; to make a sculpture of a crow in a barbed wire nest to contain his ashes, to be mounted in a real tree somewhere unknown. Terry said this last request from Guy was very hard, that when you know and love someone, the assignment was too personal and gut-wrenching to start. So the ashes are still sitting on Terry's mantle in Santa Fe, because he was just not quite ready.

... there it stayed, sort of like Excalibur
Except waiting for a tear...
... But he deserved a better tear
And I was not quite ready

"The Randall Knife"
by Guy Clark

Waylon Jennings

Waylon's personal manager, Schatzi Hageman, said Waylon detested singing that Luckenbach song that made him so much money. "He'd sing it, but always told the audience he hated it," Schatzi said. Waylon knew the Luckenbach song would be a hit but he didn't like it. It reminded him too much of Danny O'Keefe's song "Good Time Charlie Got the Blues" which he'd just recorded.

Knowing Waylon was an outlaw rebel type, Chips Moman tricked him into singing it by using reverse psychology. "Waylon," he said, "You can't sing this song because it's got your name in it!"

"I didn't think it was right for me," Waylon told a radio interviewer, "but Chips used the right approach. Luckenbach was mostly owned by Hondo Crouch. He bought it because he wanted to keep the local post office and honky-tonk open. It's a simple symbol of going home, a place to get away from things."

Waylon, a West Texas native from Littlefield, actually came to Luckenbach once for Willie's 1996 Fourth of July Picnic. He got so wrapped up in the event that he almost forgot to sing the famous song and had to be pushed back out on the stage to perform it. I was lucky to have witnessed that quintessential moment from my vantage point of selling hats on the front porch of the store.

Waylon died of diabetes in 2002. He would've been 65. I made a wreath that I set in front of the store. The ribbon draped across it said, "Waylon Jennings, Good Ol' Boy." We also made a "Waylon Wall" out of two sheets of plywood, soon to be filled with hundreds of signatures of sentiment and gratitude.

Before he died, Waylon had set up a music scholarship at The University of Texas in Hondo's name. Waylon is still celebrated at Luckenbach today. Every week, under the trees, a pickers' circle called Wacky Waylon Wednesdays is a monument made of songs thrown into the air.

"This was just a little country store when Hondo bought us," reflected Sheriff Marge. "Only farmers and ranchers who lived in the area knew about us. We went from nobody to somebody."

Our onetime town manager, who sometimes called herself "The Mare" (aka, "The Mayor") VelAnne Howell said, "I think there's something about Luckenbach that mellows people out when they get there. Sometimes you walk in a place, and you feel like you don't belong. You're not part of the in-crowd. Here, you don't have to worry about fitting in. Maybe because the place has been going on so long everybody feels like they're coming home."

Luckenbach is now owned by my son Kit Patterson, who is Hondo's grandson, and Cris Graham, Hondo's daughter.

"It's the best place to be in Texas," insists Kit, who decided to commit himself fully to the family business. "I had gotten married and it was the ideal time to invest in my heritage. Since my grandfather died (in 1976), nobody in my family has been out here on a regular basis. I'd been coming here since I was five years old, and my grandfather was telling me stories on the front porch. He'd ask me if I wanted some candy, pull out a chaw of tobacco and warn me not to swallow."

He continued, "There's a lot of history that we want to polish up, but it's kind of a Catch-22. We want to keep the town unchanged, an out-of-the-way hamlet preserving the 1880s, the 1920s and the 1940s, promoting music and humor and folklore and history. And that's what it always will be."

The Luckenbach song may have slipped from the pop charts, but in terms of endurance, it's a long-distance runner. Luckenbach will probably continue to enjoy its popularity and continue to conduct business as usual. And folks, humming the tune to "That Song," will still seek us out, all the better to get "back to the basics."

"BACK to the BASICS"

We've been so busy keepin' up with the Joneses
Four-car garage and we're still buildin' on
Maybe it's time we got back to the basics of love..."

by Chips Moman and Buddy Emmons

What are the basics, anyway? The "basics" are living a simpler lifestyle, laid back, enjoying life's ordinary little happenings, connecting with people, being authentic to one's self. Some of the "basics" experienced at Luckenbach were social gatherings, family reunions, fun in a pickup truck, the dance hall, the pickers' circle, an authentic personality like Sheriff Marge and an award-winning country singer looking for the beauty in "back to the basics of love."

Hondo's Truck

Some of the happiest moments of my life were riding in the back of my father's pickup truck cruising through the pasture. We four kids bounced around in the back hanging on for

Hondo's sudden stops, like for instance if he'd spot a deer he wanted us to see! We kept our "eagle eyes" sharpened. We called it pasture worship.

There were several trucks in Hondo's lifetime. But they were always Chevys, the paint was always faded by the sun, the fenders scratched up from the brush, and the driver's door streaked brown from spitting tobacco juice out the window into the wind. The radio was always tuned to a football game, or, if it wasn't football season, then Mexican *conjunto* music, Henry Howell's weather report, or Fibber McGee and Molly's radio show. One truck had an interesting deer hair cover over the stick shift knob—a buck scrotum. Hondo put it on fresh, and when it dried and shrank to the exact size of the knob, everyone wondered how he managed to put it on seamlessly.

There was everything you needed in the truck except a place to sit. You just had to push all the stuff over to get in. The dashboard contained a small uncatalogued archeological museum; numerous arrow heads, flint pieces—spears, axes and grindstones.

The inventory also included a deer tail, some cow tails, a gobbler's beard, opened and unopened packages of Tinsley's chewing tobacco, fat blue chalk for counting sheared sheep, penicillin syringes for infected cows, castrators and dehorners, barbed wire and bailing wire.

A half-eaten petrified piece of homemade sausage hung from the cigarette lighter. Beer cans and bottles, a cigar box of unfinished whittlings, bones, mountain laurel seeds for jewelry making, a coffee can of grass seed, a faded bathing suit, an old toothbrush, and a small package of cheese and crackers—enough sustenance for a week. Most of all this was either on the floor or seat. Hondo said he had the only truck that "spilled" when you opened the passenger door.

There were decal stickers on the dashboard, pasted over the speedometer or onto the glove compartment that revealed all you ever needed to know about the man: "Do your own thing." "Expect the unexpected." By the starter, a sign read, "Kick to start." (You had to do that to him sometimes, too.) On the rear window a sticker from an actual college, "Slippery Rock State." On the bumper, "Everybody's Somebody in Luckenbach." He once had a CB radio but it was stolen. His handle was "Buckscrape."

An excerpt from "The Truck" chapter in *Hondo, My Father*:

> *One time Hondo planned a truck drive just to say goodbye to the old cedar telephone pole high lines. The poles and crank phones were going to be replaced by buried cables and dial phones.*
>
> *"Some of those old leaning poles have such character. Let's go look at them," Hondo said one afternoon. He loved the way some of the crude knotty posts had several cross arms nailed to them. He saw beauty in the blue glass and brown porcelain insulators and the personality of sagging wires making hammocks for the mockingbirds and scissortails.*

"That's the most beautiful line in your book, Becky," Jerry Jeff called me up to tell me one day, "*sagging wires making hammocks for the mockingbirds and scissortails.*" The truck chapter inspired Jerry Jeff to write his own ode to pickups, "Pickup Truck Song."

While strumming his guitar in his typical romping country-rock style, Jerry Jeff liked to regale the audience with this opening story to his "Pickup Truck Song":

> *"My favorite part," Jerry Jeff would say as he started one of his many Hondo stories, "was when I used to go to Luckenbach and ride around with Hondo in his old green Chevy truck. The outside looked like it'd been beaten with a tire iron. Hondo'd open the door and all this junk fell out; jumper cables, snuff cans, a piece of wood he'd whittled on, oil cans. He'd say, 'Let's go to Blanco, I'll show you a shortcut!' So we left Luckenbach on FM 1376 and drove until we came to the*

Blanco turn-off at 1888 where we had to turn left. But Hondo turned even more left, on the left side of the little triangular median island. 'That's my short cut to Blanco!' he'd grin!"

Sometimes, in leading up to Jerry Jeff's truck song, the explaining was just as entertaining as the song itself. He kept up his fast talkin-strummin rhythm on the guitar as he kept the audience laughing at his Hondo stories.

"My favorite part," he'd say again, "was ridin' home from Luckenbach with Hondo one time. He'd turn the lights off and we'd ride along in the moonlight. We were on a hill when he said, 'Hey, I think it'll work here! Let's go for the coastin' record!' How far is the coastin' record so far, Hondo? 'Up to that big tree at the top of the hill.' Hondo shut the truck off and we coasted down a big grade in the road. We'd all be leanin' in the cab to make it go a little farther." The audience is laughing, baited to hear his next line. "I didn't know how serious it was. I mean, goin for a *record.* I had to try my best. Some of the fun you can have in your pickup truck!"

....I spent a few years out runnin' free
I spent two or three in New York City
And I moved back to Texas tired, hell I'd had enough
I'd go to Luckenbach on Saturdays
Cause Hondo had a way to brighten up my day
He always made me laugh when we rode in his pickup truck

We'd make a run to the county dump
We'd always wave when we saw someone
Hondo'd make up a tale as we rolled along
To the post office without fail
He'd get some chew and we'd check out the mail
And we never took the same road twice on the way back home

Well I miss grandpa and Hondo too
I really miss the things that we used to do
So last week I went out and bought me an old pickup truck
Now me and the kids spend Saturdays
We do fun things in a simple way
We love to start the day with a ride in the pickup truck

"Pickup Truck Song"
by Jerry Jeff Walker

Standing Ovation *for the* Luckenbach Dance Hall

(formerly known as Engel Halle)

In 2008, the New Braunfels Museum of Art and Music in Gruene, Texas, in affiliation with the Smithsonian Institution, featured an exhibit showcasing vintage Texas dance halls. Luckenbach's dance hall was proudly included, with a glorious narration by Texas singer-songwriter Pat Green.

Luckenbach's dance hall may be old, small, and out of the way, but thousands have harvested a crop of memories from its fertile field. Many more memories wait to be planted. The Luckenbach dance hall was recently mentioned in *Texas Monthly* as "Texas' Best Dancehall." It's definitely one of those "back to the basics" bucket-list experiences.

Formerly called Engel Hall, the dance hall was built in 1886, renovated in 1935, and has one of the best maple wood dance floors going. It has survived millions of sliding, stomping feet and at least one flood that put it two feet under water. Elizabeth Engel remembers her mother-in-law Anna baking pies to sell, and serving food on real plates (no paper plates) for the events. The dance hall was a primary social center for the entire area; the Gun Club (*Schuetzen Verein*), the men's Singing Club (*Saenger Verein*), school closings and many family reunions.

The Engels laid down strict rules, as did most of the community dance halls back then. Men had to remove their hats, and no boots were allowed. The boots would ruin the expensive new shoes of the women, and boot nails left scuff marks. "No running or hollering," said Mrs. Engel, "like they do now." Another thing, "Trucks were fined if they had no mufflers. Why don't all those motorcycles put mufflers on?" she complained about today's racket.

"Mr. Engel never put much wood into the wood stove that was in the dance hall," laughed Guich. "And for the Hunter's Dance (in November) everyone danced around with their coats on."

Verna Mae Engel mentioned the unwritten rules of her day—If you were showing your pregnancy you never danced. But you could sit on the bench and watch who your husband danced with. Also, there were never dances during Lent.

The biggest dances were on Easter Sunday night, Christmas night, and New Year's Eve.

"It was all about family," stressed Mrs. Engel. The dads taught the girls and the moms taught the boys how to dance. Mothers put their kids to sleep on pallets in the "women's dressing room," as Mrs. Engel called the tiny band's room to the left of the stage, which is now called the Hondo Hilton. Entry was 35 cents, ladies got in free. There were no tables back then, and the perimeter was lined with long benches. "I bedded my three kids down under those benches," recalled Verna Mae Engel, whose husband Danny is Benno's nephew. "I was scared there'd be scorpions in that dark side room."

Verna Mae was our first bartender when Hondo and Guich bought Luckenbach. She made excellent hamburgers for the dances. She and Danny still live in the Luckenbach community. They plowed their garden with a five-toothed plow and a mule until the Sixties. The mule knew not to step on the tomatoes.

There was a dance every six weeks, and everybody looked forward to it, and made plans to go. "You dressed up," Verna Mae said, "Like Sunday clothes. No jeans." Before there was electricity in Luckenbach, block ice was delivered once a week from Boerne and stored under a door in the saloon room floor.

The school closings were a huge all-day affair. People brought fixings to go with the barbeque sold onsite. Kids ran around and played on the rubber tire swing. The adults played scat and dominoes on the little tables in the bar. In the afternoon a program of skits, songs, recitations, and plays was presented by the students. The beautiful painted stage curtain that stays in the hall was made especially for those occasions.

The bands who most often played were Pehl's Old-Timers and the Hill Country Boys, whose Ralph Weiershausen is still among us.

Dance prices went up to sixty cents in the '60s. The bands were paid $60 a night or $10 each. They played favorites like "Beer Barrel Polka," "Red Wing," "Too Fat Polka" ("I don't want her, you can have her, she's too fat for me.") Then there was that German drinking song that translates, "All the bugs are biting except the ticks."

After beginning the dance with the grand march, everyone danced waltzes, the schottische, and polkas. There was a line dance performed side-by-side, similar to the "Cotton-Eyed Joe," called "Put Your Little Foot," a schottische-style dance.

There was also a popular dance called "Ten Pretty Girls." Verna Mae remembered the words: "Ten pretty girls in a village school, five were brunettes, four were blonde, and one was a saucy little redhead. The girls grew up, the boy left school and ended up with the saucy little redhead. And what he learned from her is that he can't have ten pretty girls anymore."

Country songs are often sad and full of lament. But it was the strong sentimentality of "Harbor Lights," said Verna Mae, that made it her's and Danny's song because they broke up and reunited to it so many times.

Herbert Boener, a delightful 86-year-old Comfort rancher recalls the Luckenbach Broom Dance. The broom dance would be

"DANCE IN SPRING"

SIGNS BEHIND BAR

reenacted if they could find brooms for a dollar; and some are still hanging from the broom rack in the bar!

"There used to be this Comfort bunch that would go over to Luckenbach for a Broom Dance," he recollected. "They had these brooms hangin' down from the ceiling in the store there and you could buy 'em for a dollar. And then they'd go in there in that dance hall and walk up to that couple that would be dancin' and *bam! bam! bam!* on the floor with the broom til the boy had to let go of the girl and, well, yes, that boy would get the girl and that other boy would get the broom! And hoo-boy! That bunch could drink that beer! And then about 12 or 18 of them would have those brooms and well, hoo-boy!"

When Hondo and Guich bought the place, the old blackboard was still on the store's weather-beaten door that read, "Dance in the Spring."

When there was a dance, it was usually on a Saturday night. Entire families came. Their children fell asleep on the benches as the parents shuffled 'til the wee hours on the well-worn pegged dance floor. Tickets were stapled to the customers' collars, allowing re-entry.

In the '70s, dance hall etiquette changed slightly. There were protests when 25-cent beer went up to 27-cents. Admission to the dances skyrocketed to two dollars. Sheriff Klaerner, 80 years old, still came, and still "had a darn good lip." It was common to see the old men dancing with six-year-old girls, girls with girls, everybody with everybody.

Hondo would sprinkle soap flakes on the floor to make for easier shuffling. Kids got braver and ran and slid across the shiny floor in between the dances. And the dress code? It went to hell. Girls showed up with their hair in those tight rollers. It made you wonder what they were saving their beauty for afterwards.

LUCKENBACH ARCHIVEW

WILLIE AND JERRY JEFF, PHOTO ON THE BAR WALL

ROBBYN DODD

DANCE HALL OVERFLOWING

Old German folk dances melted into the modern country-and-western style. Sheriff Klaerner and his entire band would wind their way across the dance floor playing "When the Saints Go Marchin' In." Soon everybody would file behind the band in a serpentine chain, singing and laughing until the clock reminded them of early morning chores.

Over time, other bands formed—the Luckenbach Jr. High Oompah Band consisting of the Fredericksburg students, and Gregg Cheser's I'd Rather Not Be Marching Band, which was assembled for the Luckenbach World Fair.

Sometimes even an electrical blowout doesn't stop the dances at Luckenbach. We're out in the country, the wiring is old; People almost expect it.

On one October Harvest dance a few years ago, all the lights and sound cut out in mid-tune. Dancers stumbled around the dance floor listening to bandleader Gary P. Nunn shout out through the darkness: "Hey, folks, hang on! It's late, but we'll find a fuse. Anyone have a fuse on 'em?"

Someone rounded up some flashlights. Someone else drove down the road and took some old-timey fuses from an old cotton gin. They came back in 30 minutes. Voila! The "Cotton-Eyed Joe" didn't miss a beat.

Animals have always found their way into the dance hall. Singer Pauline Reese traditionally brought along her horse, Blue Diamond, and her blue heeler, Baby Mae, to her gigs. They were raised on her music, with the horse in her barn where she was practicing; the dog laying in front of the kick drums. At Luckenbach, the horse just looked through the windows of the dance hall watching Pauline, and Baby Mae laid quietly at her feet on stage. One night, she rode Blue Diamond into the dance hall, to everyone's delight. So naturally, someone had to put up a sign: "no horses in dance hall."

I must end with my favorite image of our security guard, Zip Zimmerman, dancing with wife Karen at Luckenbach, with his pit bull, Skinner, following his every step. I think this image is actually immortalized on a Jerry Jeff album cover. Zip and my brother Juan Crouch were the only ones to disobey the leash law. And when Mrs. Braeutigam (a neighbor to Luckenbach) accused Skinner of killing her sheep, Zip paid her for the sheep anyway, even though he knew his dog was innocent.

We still consider our dance hall the Carnegie Hall of the Hill Country. Legendary songwriters and musicians who have sung there are too numerous to list. Prices for dances nowdays have been as high as $50 (Jerry Jeff Walker and Ray Price get the big money).

A lot of famous names have passed through. Miranda Lambert took over the whole town for a fundraiser for her favorite charity. Leon Russell, Robert Earl Keen, Los Lobos, Asleep at the Wheel, and The Mavericks are just a few of the stars who have found their way to the old dance hall with its open windows with the antique swing-up shutters. On warm nights, when the shutters are up, hundreds of fans can stand outside listening. Still "stayin' a little longer" on the bar wall is a photo of Bob Wills and the Texas Playboys, who came there in the '50s.

Songwriters are the poets of our Lone Star culture. The Luckenbach dance hall has hosted some of the Texas Heritage Songwriters Association's Hall of Famers.

"I have no idea why Texas has so much music," said 2011 Hall of Fame inductee Delbert McClinton. "I had a book, by (folklorists) John and Alan Lomax called *Folksongs of America* that showed a map of the U.S. More musical influence came out of Texas than any other state."

As music journalist John T. Davis said, "The legendary dance hall still hosts monthly dances by some of the best Texas musicians going, many of whom were toddlers when *¡Viva Terlingua!*

and 'Luckenbach, Texas' became hits. Many of the Luckenbach faithful celebrate the music, magic and memories of times they've spent in Luckenbach by returning for special occasions. As many as forty private parties are booked each year, keeping the dance hall alive almost every weekend. They come to partake of the timeless ambiance and the increasingly rare sense of being in the center of the known universe."

Ray Wylie Hubbard, who still plays at dances at Luckenbach, described the people at a Luckenbach dance like this: "They've perfected hanging out. They had their hang chops down. You step into another time. It's a bunch of people doing nothing but havin' a good time at it. The dance hall is more like a theatre. It has a deep sense of integrity to it."

Miranda Lambert *Gets* Back *to the* Basics *at* Luckenbach

In September of 2015, the whole town of Luckenbach, which had been rented out by country music star Miranda Lambert's MuttNation Foundation, was "in the pink." Pink being Miranda's favorite color—she had a pink guitar, a pink van for the rescue dogs who were the beneficiaries of the Miranda's signature charity, and pink boots were a favorite accessory among the audience. Even her retail store in her hometown of Lindale, Texas, is named The Pink Pistol.

Saving and rescuing dogs from kill shelters has been Miranda's heart-and-soul passion for over 10 years. The three-day concert was not only a fundraiser for her "Redemption Ranch" in Tishomingo, Oklahoma, but also her tradition of supporting for-adoption programs, transports, and animal shelters across the U.S.

Redemption Ranch closed when she moved from Oklahoma to Nashville. The last big event she had for the Ranch was held in Las Vegas, and, befitting Vegas, was huge and glitzy and over the top. Miranda told her mother, Bev, "The next one I want small, intimate, acoustic, toned down. I want to get back to the basics."

Bev, who selects the venues for her daughter's charity events, immediately thought, well, that would be Luckenbach. Her parents and family members are longtime fans of Willie, Waylon and the boys. She herself had been to Luckenbach dozens of times.

"We had a conference call with Kit Patterson and manager Bobbi McDaniel from Luckenbach," Bev said, "along with Miranda's promoter Brian O'Connell of Live Nation and Miranda's booking agent, Joey Lee with WME, to help put the whole package together."

The Lamberts have a deep and faithful bench of supporters and sponsors, mostly from Texas. But of course, Miranda also has a massive audience of out-of-state fans and friends who would follow her all the way to Luckenbach, off the well-beaten path. A big crowd was guaranteed.

VIP seats inside ranged from $1000 on down to $100 and sold out fast. Spots outside the dance hall went for $50. Three days of musical entertainment, free booze, a high-dollar auction, and fabulous food by Beaumont caterer Big Rich Corvell made it an event to remember.

Auction items ranged from VIP San Antonio Spurs NBA basketball tickets to an autographed guitar. But one of the most coveted items at the fundraisers was a private cantina party for 50 at the Lamberts' home. "We've had a great Texas artist, Wade Bowen, as well as Jack Ingram and also Adam Hood," said Miranda's mom afterwards. "Alone, the cantina party brought over a whopping $30,000 to the cause in Luckenbach!"

On Friday night, Gwen Sebastian of the TV talent contest, *The Voice* (she was on Team Blake, with Miranda's then-husband Blake Shelton) entertained the crowd with a dance party. Joining Miranda for her debut Luckenbach appearance were Jessi Alexander (whose hits include "The Climb," "Drink On It," "Mine Would Be You"), Jon Randall ("Whiskey Lullaby"), and Radney Foster ("A Real Fine Place to Start," "Raining on Sunday").

Miranda's songs Saturday night were inspirational and heartfelt. And there was even more magic. Who could forget little eight-year-old Riley Noon from Bandera, Texas, whose father had bought her and her mother a pair of tickets to the event for her birthday?

Riley brought with her a large pink sign, "Miranda—Can I Sing 'Automatic' with You?" Her mother, too embarrassed to take her up to the stage in front of the $1,000 seats, accepted the offer of a kind gentlemen she didn't even know to take her daughter up front. With the wave of her finger Miranda had Riley on stage sitting in her lap; her toothless grin, pink T-shirt and rhinestone sparkling boots matched Miranda's pink guitar. When you thought the moment couldn't have gotten any better Miranda waved up another little girl making it a trio of beautiful blondes in pink. They belted out the song and brought the house down. Miranda said to the little girls, "You made my day," as they exchanged hugs and embraced one another. 'Even I can't get over this!' she said.

Sunday morning was impressive. The trailers and vans full of rescue animals showed up from Houston; all air-conditioned and full of large crates, with all the comforts of home—for dogs. Rescued from high-kill centers, there was every size of canine, from puppies to grown-ups, miniatures to massive.

“All the pets came with good health certificates, were spayed or neutered, chipped with current vaccinations,” said Bev Lambert. “As a side note, I adopted a black Lab/Anatolian Shepherd there myself. His name was already Jackson but we added a middle name, Django, (Jerry Jeff’s son’s name) in honor of his Luckenbach origin!”

Manager Bobbi McDaniel wrote Kit:

> *“Well, I’ve taken about 100 pictures this morning of the dog transfer. Wow! What a crew of loving people! I’m so honored to have been a part of this one, Kit! My heart is full and my eyes are watering. Rick and Bev both told me again today how awesome we are. I’m very, very proud of our wonderful staff on this! (signed) Bobbi”*

Bobbi and Bev stood together watching as the new adoptees were loaded up by their proud new owners. “We both stood there crying,” said Bev.

¡Viva LUCKENBACH!
1993

"When I came to Luckenbach during the recording of *¡Viva Terlingua!* twenty years ago," Jerry Jeff told a CNN reporter in 1993, "I sat under those oak trees over there and wrote this ditty:

Dirt daubers humming,
See sticker burrs in your sock,
Sure signs you spent some time
In beautiful Luckenbach

One time Jerry Jeff told me, as he was writing that song, he couldn't find anything to rhyme with Luckenbach except "sock." "'Finish that up!' said Hondo. So, I did, and twenty years later I recorded it. It's called *Viva Luckenbach!*"

One day Hondo was drivin' by,
Wished he had a beer
So, he bought the place and he opened it up
And that's why we're all here!

Jerry Jeff decided it was time to pack up the band and return to Luckenbach for a new album. Time to get "back to the basics," you might say.

His longtime band, the Lost Gonzo Band, now called the Gonzo Compadres, had evolved, with some old and some new faces: John Inmon (lead guitar and vocals), Freddie Krc (drums and vocals), Bob Livingston (bass guitar and vocals), Lloyd Maines (pedal steel and dobro), Brian Piper (organ), Sweet Mary Eagan (fiddle), Craig Hillis (guitar), Michael McGeary (tambourine), Gary P. Nunn (duet vocal on "What I Like About Texas"), and Herb Steiner (pedal steel).

Jerry Jeff's son, Django, added some backup vocals and I was recorded reading two of Hondo's old Cedar Creek Clippings, "P'Likin" and "Women's Lib." It was truly a family affair. Hard to believe it had been twenty years since we'd stood in the old dance hall and watched *¡Viva Terlingua!* come to life.

In the liner notes that accompanied *Viva Luckenbach!*, Jerry Jeff reminisced:

> *"We thought we ought to use the (anniversary) occasion to make some music and, in the process, get some old friends together again. It was overdue. Time to celebrate. So, we went back to Luckenbach on October 21-22. Luckenbach worked its magic like always. It's a place that, once you're in it, feels comfortable. The reason I went there originally in '73 to make ¡Viva Terlingua! was to find a comfortable place to interact with people, to relax and make music. I decided in '73 to take my band and some mobile recording equipment to one of my favorite spots in the world: the old dance hall and beer joint/ general store owned by my friend Hondo Crouch. We laughed and cried and whooped and hollered and danced and sang, and incidentally, we made a record. It was a fine experiment. A side benefit, I found out, was the fond memories you get to keep of the event itself. The days spent with great friends making music wears well.*
>
> *"We went back in '93 for the same reasons. There we were, with all of Hondo's family sitting around in the dance hall; looking out at the faces of Hill Country friends you don't see*

enough; together with lawyers sitting next to frat rats from Dallas or Houston. Some cowboys with kids, and a dog or two. Listening to stories and songs about all of our lives and times. To get to do it twice I was really lucky. In some ways, it was nothing like 20 years ago. The hair was greyer, the music was destined for compact discs instead of scratchy old vinyl records. But for a couple of days in the midst of a glorious Texas autumn, the tiny town of Luckenbach worked its Brigadoon-like magic on all and sundry."

Hondo's "Cedar Creek Clippings," written under his pen name "Peter Cedarstacker," about a make-believe town. Cedar Creek, with its make-believe residents, reflected his satirical comments. His column was posted right next to the real news of other little towns in the local *Comfort News* society section.

Luckenbach then became the real town he could write about that had some of the same real country characters in it. Jerry Jeff included two of "Peter's" columns on the album. One was on teaching kids to "P'like" (play-like). Jerry Jeff was charmed by the magic of Hondo's studied innocence with kids, the way he would fool them to sharpen their awareness. But it was Hondo giving grown-ups permission to get in touch with their child within that was the message.

"Hondo taught me to p'like again, be a kid again," Jerry Jeff said. Hondo was a Pied Piper with kids. "He and his wife Shatzie owned and ran Camp Champions, a summer camp Hondo said, 'for over-privileged children.' Every summer I'd go up and play for the kids and visit Hondo. The camp song is set to the melody of my song 'Gypsy Songman,' with words by Becky Crouch Patterson, Hondo's daughter. Hondo said he hated kids less than most grownups."

The other article was on Women's Lib in Luckenbach, since Luckenbach had the first and only all-women chili cook-offs (or busts, as Hondo'd say).

After the album was released, Jerry Jeff and Susan invited me to go to Washington, D.C., where he'd be playing at a club, to read them again on stage. Also on the agenda was lunch at the White House with President Bill Clinton, a prize awarded to "the biggest Jerry Jeff Walker fan" who'd been to 100 concerts.

P'likin'

Mr. Spite, white, will conduct a one-day "Supposuim" for adults at the Park Side Road in Grapetown Fri. (That's short for Friday to save space in the newspaper.) I will be the instructor.

Mr. Spite has saw what a good job I've did with the Cedar Creek kids in teachin' 'em to p'like. He wants me to teach lost adults how to p'like. (P'like is when you p'like you'r a aviator, p'like you'r a engineer, or p'like you'r a nurse).

You see, children can't laugh at their ownself or their little humorous errors so to have fun some of them p'like. It's my job to teach all children to p'like.

Many adults who grow plumb up never havin' p'liked never learn to laugh at their funny ownself. This is bad said Mr Spite, white, and it sometimes causes wars. (That must mean some adults are still children.)

That's not true here in Cedar Creek. We go to the Post Office in the evenin', drink a beer, suppose we're rich and p'like we're smart and laugh at each other in the face. No one gets mad or goes on the war path 'cause we all grew up p'likin'.

Plan to attend the Supposium in Grapetown and see adults p'likin'. Suppose you come home happy. Suppose you're fat. Suppose you're a bear and p'like I throw a pie in your face! Ain't that funny and that's what life's all about.

– Peter Cedarstacker
Writer
Cedar Creek Clippings,
May 22, 1969

Remember: Fight Mental Health

Women's Lib in Luckenbach

Me and Mama walked to Luckenbach again last night and bought some flour at the post office-beer joint. Mama said she sure wished she had a car, she's so tired o'walkin' to town. I told her to get her a burro like me.

The Luckenbach Chamber of Commerce happens to meet that nite and there I was, not with my refreshment tub. We really meet every nite at the post office but when Mrs. Worstbottom, president, stands up on the apricot box and waves a beer bottle, brother, the meetin' comes to order and it's very official.

We talked of women, chili and Luckenbach and while Mrs. Worstbottom was still standin' with the beer bottle in her hand all us men became sympathizers of the "Women's Lib" movement. She smiled.

All the Luckenbach men agreed that womenfolk should have more rights like cookin' chili in a contest, scrubbin' the floors, diggin' the garden, sloppin' the hogs, guttin' the deer and milkin' the cow. They can have the babies too.

What we don't like is when women want to ride in front of the pickup. Mr Spite spoilt his'n last winter. Now, every time it rains she wants to ride in the front with her husband and dog.

Man has been pickin' on woman ever since he figured out how they weren't men, so us here in Luckenbach have decided to take up for womenfolk and let them have a place of their own to cook chili and show off where nobody'll see 'em.

– Peter Cedarstacker
Writer
Cedar Creek Clippings,
September 24, 1971

Remember: Fight the Rib

There's a place I know where we all go,
A little way down the road,
It ain't far from here, we like to sit and drink beer,
Play dominoes and tell jokes.
We've been stopping by since 49, (1849)
Ain't nothing fancy, just kids and ranches and
Clean white shirts and jeans!

Chorus:
Lots of smiling faces, little children running around,
Everybody's somebody in an old hill country town!
Dirt daubers humming, see the sticker burrs on your sock,
Sure signs you spent some time in beautiful Luckenbach!

Well, let me tell you now all about the town. . .
How it came to be. . .
In the 1800's they came in buggies
To meet and trade and buy feed.
They built the blacksmith's shop, then later on
They added the cotton gin. . .
But the old dance hall and general store's
Where it all begins and ends!

Yehaw!
In the 50's people moved to cities,
Leaving it all behind
Luckenbach closed down for good,
It just fell on a harder time
One day Hondo, driving by,
Wished he had a beer
So he bought the place and he opened it up
That's reason we're all here!

Here we go!
Lots of smiling faces, little children running around,
Everybody's somebody in an old hill country town!
Dirt daubers humming, see the sticker burrs on your sock,
Sure signs you spent some time in beautiful Luckenbach!
In beautiful Luckenbach!

"Viva Luckenbach"
by Jerry Jeff Walker

RICHARD PRUITT

HONDO'S LOVE AFFAIR WITH KIDS

The Parade

Hondo liked to celebrate his "hole in the wall town's" festivities with a parade; the Ugly Truck Contest, the Fourth of July lawnmower parade, the Jazz Fest, or the Women's Chili Bust. So, naturally, there was a parade to celebrate the making of *Viva Luckenbach!* The 200-foot one-and-only-paved road (originally named *Doppenschmidt* Avenue), with one speed bump, separated the dance hall from the post office/general store/beer joint. It was so short that the procession had to make two laps around the town to stretch the parade out. A 12-foot *Viva Luckenbach!* banner I'd made, carried by two boys, announced the parade. One car and one horse-drawn carriage brought up the rear.

Sheriff/bartender Marge Mueller sat on the hood of a Cadillac convertible with her squaw shirt spread out around her, rattlesnake earrings dangling, and tons of turquoise jewelry. As the parade marshal, Jerry Jeff rode in the car and the Gonzo Compadre band members laid back (literally), sprawled all over the trunk. My favorite "float" featured Luckenbach's official band, called the "I'd Rather Not Be Marching Band," pulled on a flatbed by the truck of Zip Zimmerman, our one-man security guard. Everyone's kids filled the back of his truck.

Sheriff Hugo Klaerner, (a real sheriff), known for his toe-tappin' German Oompah band, played at the horse races and many a Luckenbach dance. He was so big he was barely able to fit the big bass tuba horn around himself. It was the nucleus of this band that, reassembled, added some Fredericksburg school band members, and renamed itself the "Luckenbach High School Marching Band" for our first Luckenbach World's Fair (you can see their picture in the bar).

Then the remnants of *that* band and other stragglers formed the afore-mentioned "We'd Rather Not Be Marching Band." It was casually conducted with a long limp peach twig by Gregg Cheser, and pulled by Zip's truck and flatbed trailer. The ensemble was a horn band made up of the young and old, the tired and has-been, mostly all of German descent. A lopsided Cinzano umbrella teetered over some of them. To add to the pitiful ambiance, the trailer always had a flat tire. And if it didn't, someone sabotaged it to keep up the flat tire tradition. The band had played in every major parade in Fredericksburg, and now was the main float at Luckenbach for Jerry Jeff's *Viva Luckenbach!* album release party.

If there had been more parade entries than this there wouldn't be any spectators left to watch the parade. Going over the speed bump in Luckenbach usually broke a horn player's lip. So, Zip had to be a careful driver. Zip remembered being complemented on his smooth driving for the vulnerable horn players. "How'd I do?" he'd asked them. "Well, Sip (they always called him Sip) I didn't bust my lip once-st!"

After the parade, Zip said he'd continue driving the band-laden trailer around town for "drive-by polkas." They'd stop at Atldorf and Oma Koock's and play "Beer Barrel Polka" or "She's Too Fat for Me." Finally, after two hours of this, the police told them to go home because they were causing traffic jams and they had 35 people on their trailer. Even Zip needed a bouncer at times. We need to revive this fun and funny tradition of the "We'd Rather Not Be Marching Band" as one of Luckenbach's originals.

"Hondo changed my life and influenced my music," Jerry Jeff told the CNN reporter. "I'm more mature, hopefully, and more mellow. I was pretty wild when I first came down here (from New York to Texas). Hondo got me to slow down, lighten up, enjoy life.

"He reminded us again what he liked about Luckenbach. The reason I came down here to Luckenbach: I was butting heads with the music biz and I wanted to feel comfortable doing an album. You have a memory here you otherwise wouldn't have. It's getting involved with the people." The last chorus of the last song on the album says it all:

I hope everybody here is really feeling fine
Speaking for myself and the band, we had a hell of a time
We laughed and cried and we carried on
And everybody sang the singalong
We had a good time, time that we're movin on

"Movin' On"
by Jerry Jeff Walker

Another song, by Tommy Alverson, expresses the same mentality and ambience of "Why Luckenbach?":

Country music's all the rage these days
Nashville's grinning from ear to ear
I don't think I'm showin my age
But I don't like what I hear
You know we saw this happen once before
And the answer's so very plain to see.
We'll go back to a place where less is more
And it's a long way from Tennessee

... The best in life and music still come free
We'll sit around the campfire once again
And pass around that Sangria Wine
We'll sing all might with our Gonzo friends
Texas music suits us just fine

Chorus:
It's time we started lookin back to Luckenbach
Hondo's gone but his spirit remains
We'll shout Viva Terlingua *down in Luckenbach*
Wash our souls in the Hill Country Rain

"Lookin' Back To Luckenbach"
by Noel Clement & Tommy Alverson

MAKING OF ¡*VIVA TERLINGUA*! ALBUM.

(LEFT TO RIGHT) JUAN CROUCH, CRIS GRAHAM, JERRY JEFF AND SUSAN, GONZO COMPADRES BAND, BECKY PATTERSON.
COURTESY OF JERRY JEFF WALKER

WILLIE'S COMIN'!

Listen to my song and if you want to sing along
It's about where I belong, Texas.

by Willie Nelson

The *Great* Domino Confrontation

Hondo was picking up beer cans after the beer joint closed one evening in 1975. "Willie's comin' tomorrow, but you can't tell anybody," Hondo told Maggie Montgomery. "It's a secret!"

Hondo had invited Willie to the inaugural Luckenbach Domino Tournament, an extravaganza that consisted of only four contestants; Willie and his partner and lifelong amigo, Zeke Vernon, a real estate broker and resident of the pool hall that Willie's Mom and Pop Nelson ran in Austin for a while. To defend Luckenbach's honor, Sheriff Marge had rounded up Lightning Louie Gerhardt, almost 90 years of age, but who still had a sharp mind and keen hands, and Calvin Steubing, who admitted to being over 60.

The night before, Hondo had raked up the bottle caps that over the years had made a crunchy carpet on the dirt yard outside. He

HONDO WATCHES OVER WILLIE, LIGHTNING LOUIS, AND CALVIN STEUBERG

put up a hand-lettered butcher paper sign on the outside bar wall announcing the tournament between Willie's Pool Hall (crudely spelled "Haul" by Hondo) VS. "The Whole City of Luckenbach," which only needed Lightning Louie and Steubing.

Willie's expected arrival was 3:00 p.m. At the crack of three no one was in the town except Hondo, Sheriff Marge, and Maggie. Shortly thereafter, a little silver Mercedes pulled up to the hitchin' post at the side of the store. It was Willie. Maggie was so nervous serving him a beer that she slid all the way down the bar counter to him, but she'd forgotten to open it.

Hondo's philosophy to keep the visitation a secret worked. Yeah, sure it did. Word spread like wildfire. By 4:00 p.m. you couldn't find a parking spot within two miles in any direction of Luckenbach. Even though Hondo tried to keep it a secret, two thousand Willie Nelson fans showed up. People were hanging out of the trees over the little domino table outside.

Gerhardt and Steubing won the best four out of seven games before Willie could say, "Funny how games slip away." Zeke cried out for a rematch at the pool hall saying, "Well, I guess we can play for a couple hundred dollars a game!" "Fifty cents!" commanded Lightning Louie. The two old timers had roared to victory as Willie roared out of town in his silver Mercedes.

Willie loved Luckenbach and Hondo. He'd return unannounced, to hang around the pickers' circle, or hear Hondo recite "Luckenbach Moon" to him. So, Willie's idea to have his famed Fourth of July Picnic in the heart of the rural Texas Hill Country made Luckenbach the ideal destination. There, through the years, the harmonious haven of Luckenbach, which had become a shrine for musicians, was the place to express and celebrate both the people and the music that define Texas cultures.

"Willie embodied the Luckenbach spirit, that everybody is somebody," said one-time Luckenbach manager, Neal Brown.

Luckenbach is a place that bolsters up not only good music, but also exists as a free and independent spirit in its own right. Willie held five vastly successful July Fourth Picnics there, from 1995–1999. "The first thing a lot of people ask when they walk into Luckenbach is 'When was the last time Willie was here?' as if he drops in to play dominoes all the time," Brown said. "And we usually say, 'Oh, the Fourth of July.'"

The Fourth of July Picnics

Willie, a gypsy in relentless pursuit of the definitive portrayal of American life, hosted his first Fourth of July Picnic in Dripping Springs, Texas, in 1972. Fifteen thousand people showed up to help Willie wish America a proper happy birthday. The show bombed financially, but it begat a Lone Star holiday tradition.

The event enticed entertainers from all the spectrums of the country music scene, from Bill Monroe to Kris Kristofferson, and showcased the raw Texas hybrid of country and rock 'n roll that was rising to define a culture of limitless possibility and exciting creative endeavor. National magazines like *Rolling Stone* dubbed Willie Nelson's Fourth of July Picnic "the Woodstock of Texas," as it would forever change the view of local entertainment and set a precedent for untamed cultural and musical innovation.

"It all started out as a bunch of people and pickers, with nobody expecting to get paid, everyone just getting together to pick and celebrate," Willie's promoter Tim O'Connor said of the first event at Dripping Springs. "It developed over the last 30 years

FOURTH OF JULY CROWD OF 13,000 IN LUCKENBACH TEXAS

into a state-wide anthem on the Fourth of July brought to you by Willie."

"Willie's picnics are like goin' to the Land of Oz, they're always interesting and fun," said Ray Wylie Hubbard.

Zip Zimmerman, Luckenbach's Chief of Security recalls his favorite memory of the Picnics at Luckenbach. "It was when I had to be Secret Service for Willie. I saw a Texas Ranger sitting at the entrance gate in his lawn chair. He had on his typical khakis and starched white shirt. 'How many are there of you?' I asked."

"Just me," he answered. "You know, one party, one Ranger." That one Texas Ranger at the gate checked 13,000 people coming through, screening for any ice chests, alcohol, umbrellas, glass items, pets, weapons, video cameras. Luckenbach was a special fragile treasure and everyone always showed respect for the antique town.

People had to walk in. No cars were allowed. They stood or sat shoulder to shoulder next to each other over a three-acre field; a sea of quivering humanity. Misting water hoses cooled people off. There was a first-aid tent for heat stroke victims. There were many food and lemonade stands, along with beer trucks stashed with a week's worth of beer.

Zip said, "Luckenbach's five Willie Nelson picnics were all success stories. For the first one, the promoters had a meeting with the Department of Public Safety beforehand. They warned all the law and security personnel that, for a crowd of 15,000, they were statistically expecting 900 arrests. Jails in Fredericksburg, Mason, Llano, Kendall County and Johnson City were standing by ready to house any troublemakers. There were only 90 arrests." Zip and Kit Patterson were congratulated by the DPS. The only vehicle allowed in the town for this event was a school bus jail for PIs (intoxicated partygoers) to sleep off their fun until they sobered up.

One of the yearly picnic volunteers, Robyn Turner, an ardent Willie fan, remembered the friendly ambience and the spell that those music picnics cast on her:

> *"The Willie Fourth of July Picnic always transformed Luckenbach into a larger-than-life venue, both literally and figuratively, from pushing the physical boundaries to form a music venue for 13,000 in a big field, to bringing in volunteer staff of locals who sustained the Luckenbach homegrown flavor until the last fans went home at dark-thirty.*
>
> *"The whole place was Texana fantastical that day with no way to improve on anything from any angle. The heat, the slow pace, the mellow mood. One day when the sun was beating down and the music was at its peak, Bill Bell (silversmith maestro of Willie's silver dollar coin belts) invited me to step into Willie's bus to meet him. I froze! While I had seen Willie no fewer than 50 times at various venues, had hugged his neck after a small benefit at the VFW Hall in Fredericksburg, and later on stage at the Broken Spoke, had caught red bandanas that he hurled at me from other stages, had blown back*

kisses between songs, had stood in line for autographs on my hat my belt and my skin—I couldn't bring myself to step up into the 'Honeysuckle Rose' bus on that hot afternoon in Luckenbach. Why? All I know is that at the Luckenbach Willie Picnics, everything was already magic, just like Willie had been in my eyes every time I had seen him perform throughout the decades.

"Perhaps I was afraid of breaking the spell. I was not prepared personally to converse with a legend. It'd be like meeting the Wizard of Oz behind the curtain. Regardless, to this day, Willie and Luckenbach are two brands of Texas magic that always came together in the Hill Country—each year at those legendary Luckenbach Fourth of July Willie Nelson Picnics."

Willie usually brought about 30 performers for 10–13 hours of entertainment. Tickets were $25.00. Here are a couple of lineups for '96 and '99: (They're just a sample because many performers have made repeat appearances.)

1996 Willie Nelson and Family, Waylon Jennings, Leon Russell, Robert Earl Keen, Steve Fromholz, Asleep at the Wheel, Ray Price, Kimmie Rhodes, Little Joe y la Familia, Titty Bingo, Billy Walker, Jesse Dayton, Jubal Clark, Paula Nelson, Doc Mason, Eva Mason, Aaron Allen, the Antone's Blues Band, Jimmy Lee Jones, Maggie Montgomery, Monte Montgomery, Ray Wylie Hubbard, Billy Joe Shaver, Craig Dillingham, Supersuckers, 8 ½ Souvenirs, Twisted Willie, The Geezinslaws, Kinky Friedman, Freddie Powers, Gary P. Nunn.

1999 Willie Nelson and Family, Asleep at the Wheel, Razzy Bailey, Bells of Joy, Tab Benoit, Bobby Boyd, Johnny Bush, Cowjazz, Donnie Fritts, Steve Fromholz, Larry Gatlin, The Geezinslaws, Pat Green, Claude Grey, Ray Wylie Hubbard, Janis Ian, Jimmy Lee Jones, Jackie King, Lil' Joe and Son, Mark David Manders, Doc Mason and Ava, Bill McDavid, Monte Montgomery, Paula Nelson, Derek O'Brien, Freddy Powers, Ray Price, Kimmie Rhodes, Lee Rocker, Leon Russell, Billy Joe Shaver, Sisters Morales, Pump Skully, Supersuckers, Titty Bingo.

PICNIC FANS

Willie has traditionally been generous and charitable with his causes. Take, for example, his long-running series of annual Farm Aid benefits, held to support the family farmers of America, those tillers of the soil whose crops were at the mercy of the weather and man-made challenges.

Clayton Knopp, a local farmer, rented out his fields just down the road to provide parking for the picnickers each year. The revenues produced from the annual event helped the Knopp family cushion an ongoing economic struggle that is all too familiar to many farmers. "I made more in that one day than I did in ten years of farming," Knopp said.

Willie Nelson's Farm Aid program has helped out family farmers like Knopp for the past 14 years. His Fourth of July Picnic rendered additional revenue for local Hill Country farms which have followed Knopp's initiative in renting out their fields for the Picnic.

FOURTH OF JULY PICNIC POSTER BY LEGENDARY ARMADILLO WORLD HEADQUARTERS ARTIST JIM FRANKLIN

"There's just no way anymore," he said after the last concert. "I've got to plant a couple more acres this year just to keep farming. Ole' Willie, he has always been there for us and it's a blessing he's gone as far as he has. He knows you don't run a man down; you help people. He's helped me a whole lot."

His annual event also helped sustain a renewal of rural Luckenbach, in spite of the wear and tear 13,000 fans inflicted on it. The '96 Willie bash financed $25,000 to upgrade the septic system, with enough left over for a new tin roof on the leaky dancehall, along with a sorely-needed electrical rewiring job.

Luckenbach, in turn, was unique in compensating the Gillespie County Sheriff's Department, contributing to the EMS of Blanco, the Volunteer Fire Departments of Pedernales, Fredericksburg and Stonewall, and to civic organizations around Fredericksburg.

For a few years I had a hat business called "Hondo's Hats" which were a collection of new or old cowboy hats with character, like Hondo wore, all of them beat up, antiqued and soulful. I rehabilitated and adorned them, and named them after the characters who wore them in films. I was selling them off the front porch of the store during the Picnics.

One year I made one for Emmylou Harris and took it to her trailer. I'd made a felt one for our Luckenbach local, Maggie Montgomery, laced the brim with ribbon, with punched star vent holes on the sides and embellished it with a horsehair hat band and stampede string. She threw it up to Willie on stage one time at a concert in Austin and he never threw it back, kept it; wore it everywhere. I even saw him wearing it on *The Tonight Show*, and in photos in several periodicals.

But the other hat I made especially for him at the last Luckenbach Picnic was a head-turner. It was a wide-brimmed Guatemalan straw, almost sombrero-like, similar to the one he wore in the movie version of *Red-Headed Stranger*. My hat partner, Russ Cox, and I met Willie in his "Honeysuckle Rose" bus to give it to him, but when he put it on his head it was too big. He looked like Baby New Year.

Graciously and tactfully he said, "That's OK. We all wear the same hat size in Luckenbach," implying that no swollen egos or big heads were welcome here. Hondo's philosophy of humor when he said, "We're all the same size," was to put the big guy down and pull the little guy up. Willie just put a bandana on his head to anchor the hat and wore it anyway. Willie's comment about "everyone's the same size in Luckenbach" truly expresses the common denominator we admire and share with this genuinely humble and gracious man.

Pic-Nix

The five picnics ran smoothly, with few problems of any note. It was mostly a mellow crowd. But there would not be a sixth. Because some festival in San Antonio went awry, the "Mass Gathering Act," a new law in Gillespie County, put guidelines around events held outside city limits for safety of the people gathering for large events.

In 2000, the new law was modified to limit people at any given outdoor event to 10,000; Willie had had 13,000 at Luckenbach the year before. And likewise, events were limited to five hours' duration; Willie's lasted twelve. The new law also demanded prearranged contracts for all entertainers. The Mass Gathering Act all but directly outlawed an event such as Willie's Picnic, where musicians have always had an open forum to jump up and join in on the pickin', *by mandating prearranged contracts* with all performers prior to applying for the now-necessary permit.

"Most people don't even have a contract, they just come because they want to pick," promoter Tim O'Connor said. "You never know who Willie meets on tour and invites at the last minute, and that's part of the excitement of it, you never know who's going to show up."

Luckenbach actually applied for and received the permit, courtesy of Gillespie County Judge Stroeher, but it could be pulled at any time. Willie and Tim O'Conner weren't willing to put themselves at the mercy of a judge who could yank the permit at any time if, in his view, all rules weren't met.

The disappointment was great for everyone involved; Luckenbach, with its identity, and Gillespie County, economically. In some peoples' minds, it seemed that time had clouded the memory of the spirit that once gave the town its magical allure and inspired the classic hit, "Luckenbach, Texas (Back to the Basics of Love)".

Many locals pointed out the irony of the fact that it was "That Song" that put Luckenbach in the national limelight as a place of charm and freedom, yet Willie can't return to his own shrine of free expression to celebrate a day of liberty due to county legislation.

Tim O'Connor said, "It is disheartening when an event meant to celebrate the freedoms of our country on the Fourth of July, with musicians and Texas citizens coming together to enjoy those freedoms, would be shut down by our own government officials. I am very frustrated that they would insult a man of Willie Nelson's stature in this manner and stop an event that has been successful not only throughout the state for over 30 years, but more importantly in the same location, Luckenbach, for almost five years.

"I think it's an insult to Willie, I think it's an insult to the people of Texas, and I think it's most unfortunate that it happens to be on the Fourth of July."

Since 2000, Willie has held Picnics in Fort Worth, Austin and elsewhere in Texas. The tradition continues but, sadly, Luckenbach is no longer part of it.

TOM WILKES

¡*VIVA TERLINGUA*! COVER ART—HONDO AT BAR DOOR

LUCKENBACH HOWITZER CANNON AND FIRETRUCK

COTTON-EYED-JOE

PICKER'S CIRCLE

BIKE RALLY

GARY P. NUNN

ROBBYN DODD

RAY WYLIE HUBBARD

ROBBYN DODD

STOVE SESSIONS.
BRADLEY KOPP,
RICHARD BOWDEN,
BOB LIVINGSTON.

JOE ELY

ROBBYN DODD

NIGHT ENCHANTMENT, THE DANCEHALL AND STORE

ROBBYN DODD

BILLY JOE SHAVER

ROBBYN DODD

LEON RUSSELL

LOS LOBOS AND TEXMANIACS SIGN

ROBBYN DODD

LOS LOBOS AND TEXMANIACS

ROBBYN DODD

DALE WATSON
AND RAY BENSON

ROBBYN DODD

ROBBYN DODD

RAUL MALO, THE MAVERICKS

ABBEY ROAD AND SHOOTER JENNINGS

ROBBYN DODD

WAYLON'S WREATH

ROBBYN DODD

NELLIE WILSON AND WILLIE NELSON

RUTH NUNN

CRIS GRAHAM AND WILLIE

The LUCKENBACH MONTHLY MOON CHRONICLES

Celebrating "The Everybodies"

The *Luckenbach Monthly Moon*, founded in the '70s, is published mainly to announce the calendar of events for Luckenbach festivals, as well as shows in the dance hall and the beer joint. But more importantly, it reveals the true fabric and character of the people with whom it networks; from the staff to the grassroots "everybodies" out there.

Here's a peek into the life and laughter it stirs up, with a few feature articles, headlines and letters. The *Moon* is sub-titled with one of Hondo's quotes: *People can't believe we have such a big moon for such a small town; Dedicated to Peter Cedarstacker.* Cost 25¢. Staff editors have ranged from John Raven, Maggie Montgomery and Barbara Mann to Alex Cortez. Featured writers included me and Maggie Montgomery; other contributors featured include poet Walt Perryman, Dave Thomas and Mac McIntyre, and the immortal Peter Cedarstacker and his "*Cedar Creek Clippings.*"

On the Road Again Entire Town Shows Off
September, 1995

The entire town of Luckenbach (almost) motored to Bee Cave, just outside of Austin, two Sundays ago to show off at a chili cook off held at the Back Yard. They often go there to hear Willie and other famous musicians in concert, but this time they took a replica of the Luckenbach Store and some hay bales and p'liked we were at Luckenbach. The store front was constructed by Zip and Varm (famous construction types) and created through the magic brushes of Allegani Jani (formerly of Hot Pants Chili, now of Hot Flash Chili), world champion chili cook and Woody (famous artist types). They came home with a First Place Trophy for Showmanship that was presented to "that crazy bunch from Luckenbach." This group of fun lovers took the prize competing under the guise of the Luckenbach Ladies Lynchin' League, "We Always Get Our Man," and the Feral Bachelors of Luckenbach. Good work gang and thanks!

Luckenbach Royalty Mr. and Mrs. Pat Green
June 10, 2000

Kory and Pat Green dance their first dance as husband and wife in the legendary Luckenbach Dance hall, on Saturday, June 10, 2000, while being serenaded from the stage by another representative of Luckenbach royalty... Django Cody

> *Walker, son of Luckenbach legends Susan and Jerry Jeff Walker! Django is a student at the Liverpool Institute for the Performing Arts. Django, at 6' 6", has inherited not only his father's stature, but looks and talent, too!*

Thus read the announcement of the Greens' wedding at Luckenbach in the *Moon*. Pat, a Texas music icon, and considered "royalty" at Luckenbach, is a three-time Grammy nominee. His special relationship with the dance hall is that not only has he played concerts there, he wrote a song, "Dancehall Dreamers". He also worked with author Luke Gilliam and photographer Guy Rogers, III on the 2008 book, *Pat Green's Dance Halls and Dreamers*, about Texas' legendary vintage dance halls and the musicians who made them great. Those venerable venues serve as landmarks to the musicians in their rise to fame, as epitomized by Jerry Jeff Walker and the legendary music recorded right here in Luckenbach.

Equally essential to the story are the dance hall owners, bartenders, security and fans. Pat's not only married to wife Kory, but to the Texas vintage dance halls as well. His Top Ten list of Texas Dance Halls includes: Luckenbach, Gruene Hall, the Bandera Caberet, Coupland Inn, Schroeder Hall, Stubb's Bar-B-Q, Billy Bob's Texas, John T. Floore's Country Store, the Sons of Hermann Halle, and the late, great Saengerhalle.

Along with Jerry Jeff's son Django Walker singing at the wedding, fellow Texas singer-songwriter Cory Morrow also performed. Of playing at the dance hall, he said, "Every artist who plays at Luckenbach becomes touchable, approachable."

An excerpt from Pat Green's book, *Pat Green's Dance Halls and Dreamers*, reveals why he obviously chose Luckenbach for his wedding:

> *The places that meant most to me were the places I would go and hang out and watch music. One of those places was Luckenbach. The excitement comes from the peoples' personal connections and memories of these beer joints. The dance halls have the*

feeling of the old hardwood floors and the history to go along with it. Look at the pictures on the wall (in the bar).

I remember seeing Jerry Jeff Walker on the cover of Texas Monthly standing in the Luckenbach dance hall door. I wanted to go there. I want people to be aware of how great this scene is and what's happening in Texas music; to have an appreciation for where this music started. Everybody felt the same when Robert Earl Keen would come to Luckenbach and we would crowd around the windows if it was too crowded to get inside.

These dance halls are comfort places for me. The connection between myself and the crowd seems like it's right in your face. Places like Luckenbach are so old and people write songs about them. Those are the kinds of places that deserve reverence and respect. I'm more proud of my song 'Dancehall Dreamers' than any other I've written.

Steve *and* Harley, Luckenbach's Short-Lived *Radio* Show
June, 2001

Luckenbach's come a long way since Hondo and Kathy bought this sleepy hamlet. Amenities have been upgraded ever so gradually: The powers-that-be have installed several indoor flushing toilets; changed the cigar box to a cash register; the 1929 tire swing has been updated to a 1950 tire swing, and there's even a credit card machine and ATM machine.

But nothing is as high tech in terms of going way out on an Internet limb as the day we decided to launch Luckenbach's own radio show webcast, The *Steve and Harley Show*. Our 20-foot tall airmail pole, our retired parking meter, our Texas flagpole are all standin' ever so tall so as to feel these new satellite waves bouncin' around.

If you haven't heard of the funniest guys in Texas radio, Steve Alex and Harley Balew, you are in for some belly laughs and feel goods. They come close to being an intellectual (at times) Tuna, Texas. What makes them so Texas is... they have a sense of our rugged individualism. They know how to pronounce all those unusual Texas towns, too (like Mexia). Which, for all our out-of-state visitors, is "Ma-hay-ya."

I've heard a sample of their already well-honed show. It's ear food with a lot of flavors. They've got a smorgasbord from grits to sourdough. They spotlight a featured Texas musician, rummage in Hondo's archival corner, flash back to "Looking back in Luckenbach." There's annoying prank calls where they're pulling someone's leg, humorous stories, and a roving mike that picks up our grassroots real people out here.

These guys have been to Dallas, New York, and Big Flat and came back saying, "They don't amount to much." After two years and much practice perfecting their *Texas Morning Show*, they have pooled their wisdom and realize they are finally ready for the big time... Luckenbach! Their most hilarious contribution was that they imitated Texas presidential candidate Ross Perot on the Luckenbach answering machine menu. You cannot figure out fact from fiction. They both told me they started out as black children. They met when the State of Texas sent them both to a penal institution for wayward kids. It was there they studied radio.

Steve and Harley wanted me to know this about them: "We understand Hondo's humor. It's truth, playfulness, not taking himself so seriously. What did Mark Twain, Jesus, and Hondo have in common? They aimed at people who take themselves too seriously, who are shams, puffed up, controlling. They teach us to have fun again in this mean ole world. We encourage people, and try to make them laugh."

How Much *Food* Could a Chuckwagon Chuck If *a* Chuckwagon Could Chuck *Food*? (All 'n Nall)

April, 2005

One of Luckenbach's most loved Regulars is Tom Nall, chuckwagon cook *extraordinaire*, founder of the Republic Brand of tequila and whiskey that comes in Texas-shaped bottles. Tom is featured in the book *Texas Men—Big Guns, Rising Stars and Cowboys*. An aside note, he's in the *Guinness Book of World Records* for eating the most corn tortillas... 74 in 30 minutes.

Have you been lucky enough to be around his chuckwagon that comes to Luckenbach, usually on Texas Independence Day? I have.

Tom, whose wagon was sponsored by 2-Alarm Chili, and Gerry Self, sponsored by Jardine's Salsas, were the centerpieces with their authentic rigs for three days, dishing out delicious food, fun, and camaraderie in spite of the hardships of cooking with heavy iron pots.

Tom's cowboy cooks are a faithful team that have been doing chuckwagon cooking at Luckenbach together for eight or nine years. The 2-Alarm Chuckwagon Gang is Tom's brother Marc Nall ("Blue"), Jim Tugman ("Bob Wire"), Rhonda and Jack Potter ("Yukon Jack" or "Jackpot"), Don and Leslie Rayburn (eternal Luckenbach newlyweds), and Ted Parsons ("Rocky Caliche"). The 2-Alarm Gang all melded at the Ladies Only Chili Cook-off here at Luckenbach back in '96. Tom was asked to cook 50 pounds of chili to serve guests and tourists, since the chili cooks themselves swiftly ran out of their meager samples.

TOM NALL:
FROM TERLINGUA TO LUCKENBACH

ANDY REISBURG

TOM NALL AT TERLINGUA

Tom was also a regular at Terlingua, out in far West Texas chili championship territory. He was a natural PR icon and became sponsored by Wick Fowler, who invented 2-Alarm Chili, as well as the Terlingua chili cook-offs. Tom and food man Jim Tugman teamed up to cook chili for food shows dedicated to the cowboy theme; and also dedicated to the charity ALS Association. ALS, or, Amyotrophic lateral sclerosis, which most famously took ballplayer Lou Gehrig, was also the disease that killed Wick Fowler.

Tom is much more than a colorful figure at romantic-looking food shows. Tried and true, he's the real deal. After the purchase of the wagon and a team of Percheron draft horses, Tom bought Conejo Ranch in Colorado, which became a base camp for classic Western trail rides. From Conejo Ranch, with mutual friends and neighbors, the Quinlans of Chama, New Mexico, and Andie Cominie, a *City Slicker* movie-type trail ride organizer from Texas, Tom was the functioning horse-drawn chuck wagon on the trail rides.

He also provided food for the Quinlan cattle drive every spring. The Quinlan Ranch of 12,000 acres provided grazing for 700 head of cattle. Twenty-five trail riders herded these cattle through the Archuleta National Forest from the Quinlan Ranch to Colorado. The 70-mile trip took one week, going 10 miles a day. Tom cooked three meals a day for 30 people and for 100 at the trip's end.

Tom's chuckwagon, based on the model invented by cowman Charles Goodnight, is authentic. It has a coffee grinder attached, a shaving mirror and girlie photos. With a shortage of firewood on the range, a "coonie," or cowhide was stretched under the wagon to carry cow or buffalo chips ("prairie coal") to burn. The cook was called a "coosie" (from the Spanish word *cocinero*). Have you ever heard of "Son-of-a-Bitch" Stew? It's a menudo-type stew made up of cow organs: marrow, guts, liver, tongue, sweetbreads, brains and heart—fired up with a lot of chile pequins. He cooks that.

Tom and his gang slept in authentic cowboy trail tents of canvas and cedar poles for three nights when at Luckenbach. The "*taco de ojo*" (food for the eye) is Tom and his cowboy cooks. Tom wears knee-high yellow boots with antique spectacles. All have great hats and silk windrags around their necks tied with Tom's signature square square-knot. They don yellow slickers when it rains. Setting all traditional cowboy correctness aside, Rocky pops open a huge black and white striped Wilson tennis umbrella with a peppy cry, "Let's Cowboy Up!" when the showers commence. The gang huddles over the steaming pots, pouring rain water off the coals banked on the lids and trying to keep the fires going. There's something fabulous in every Dutch oven, the classic cowboy cast iron stewpot that can cook everything from enchiladas to peach cobbler.

Tom's cooking is a mix between classic cowboy favorites with *avant garde* Western cuisine. The menu here, in his own words, features some of his special products:

> *Of course, a pot of 2-Alarm Chili will be on the fire all weekend. We'll prepare garlic-stuffed pork tenderloin basted with Cajun Creole mustard and Tiger Sauce. Yukon smoked potato salad tossed in French vinaigrette; red cabbage cored and then the cavity filled with blue cheese dressing, wrapped in foil and placed on hot coals to steam; elk steak fajitas grilled and served with flour tortillas; calf fries, a Texas delicacy, their testicles, (aka "mountain oysters"), battered and dipped in Try Me Cajun Hot Sauce prior to serving, marinated chicken parts grilled over hot coals. Dessert, of course is No Pudge Chocolate Brownies and Yukon Whiskey Cake.*

At Tom's chuckwagon we also feast on stories—ones we've never heard, repeats of ones we've heard before. One story I had never heard before was told by Tom. I'm always hearing a new Hondo story:

> *Place: Bandera, Texas, in Arkie Blue's Silver Dollar saloon, standing at a urinal in a men's restroom next to Hondo. Upon*

seeing two dimes in the urinal, Hondo reaches into his pocket and throws in about 75¢ in coins. Upon leaving, Hondo gathers up all the coins. "Why did you do that?!" was Tom's obvious question. Hondo's retort, "You didn't think I'd stick my hand in there for just 20¢, did you?"

Thank you to Gerry, Tom and the 2-Alarm Gang for bringing us some romance of the Old West past. We appreciate your inconvenience to haul, fix, and feed us lucky observers and tasters. Here's to all the camp cooks, alias biscuit-shooters, pot rasslers, belly-cheaters, grub-spoilers, dough-punchers, and beanmasters.

Virgil Holdman: *Our* One-Man Band
June, 2009

"Everybody's Somebody in Luckenbach" is a traveling saying Guich Koock and Hondo came up with. When it comes to our ambassador of Luckenbach, Virgil Holdman, the saying becomes "Virgil's Everybody in Luckenbach." He is our one-man band staff member. You've probably seen him on duty somewhere on the town's property.

Virgil is a vision: long, thin body, long, thin handlebar mustache, long, thin pigtail, and long, tall boots. When he opens his mouth, out falls cheery "howdys" and corny *Hee-Haw*-type lines wrapped in a Texas accent that pinpoints him specifically as being from Abilene. And a musical laugh that will make you laugh your ownself just hearing it.

You never know whether to believe him or not. He says he went to sixth grade from 1966 to 1971, but missed graduation because he was on jury duty. Virgil was a rodeo cowboy in high

ROBBYN DODD

VIRGIL HODMAN: OUR ONE-MAN BAND

school until 1980. Would you believe—doing the world's most dangerous extreme sport—riding bulls! Now he's content just shooting the bull.

"I've dealt cards in Bullhead City, Nevada," Virgil says as he recounts the various hats he's worn, "and worked in uranium mines in Milan, New Mexico. I've put in water lines in the high desert of California, right behind the Roy Rogers Museum."

As I was wandering around in the general store one day where Virgil was his usual happy, folksy self behind the sales counter, I hear, "Here's your change, sir. And I didn't even have to take off my boot to find it!" Another customer comes in and asks how Virgil's doing. "If I was a dog my tail'd be waggin' and I'd be chasin' that cat over there."

Here are Virgil's jack-of-all-trades Luckenbach job titles: HOOSER (Head Of Our Security; Enuf Riots), ALMOST (Assistant Luckenbach Manager Of The Store), Member of the SS (one of the Store Salesmen), A MOB (Assistant Manager Over the Bar), COB (Counter Of Beer, inventory).

But Virgil's greatest gift is greeting people as they, finally, make it to Luckenbach and walk through the store doors. "These doors are the gateway to Luckenbach," Virgil says. "If there ain't nobody pickin' or singin', I entertain them with my corny jokes and maybe brighten their day up. I love the people that come from all over, have fun with them. I greet them with a smile and a handshake."

As I was leaving the store some unwitting newcomers were coming in, probably touring motorcycle couples. Virgil welcomed them too: "You ladies come with your dads?" Then, still within earshot, I heard more. Pointing to one of the store items, a taxidermed armadillo laying on its back holding a bottle of beer, Virgil asked them, "Y'all seen the Himalayan Armadillo?" He immediately baited their curiosity, "We found him a layin' in the road!"

The staff members at Luckenbach are the greatest. They are usually over-qualified, ex-CEOs, and nearly all the bartenders also sing. They have to love being here because it's either lonesome or a mob.

Abbey Road's Road *to* Luckenbach
December, 2011

"Thank God you're on this earth!" cried famed blues musician W.C. Clark with tears in his eyes. "Or I never woulda seen or played in Luckenbach!" He was talking to Abbey, our Events Manager, who invented the Blues Festival at Luckenbach. Abbey, who doesn't have a last name, but is called "Abbey Road," by all, has created some of Luckenbach's most successful and amazing events in the last seven years, simply due to her acute observations and love of Luckenbach. "One day the wind blew, the stars realigned and I found myself getting lost in Luckenbach," Abbey said.

"I love my job. I wake up every day wondering how I can get the world—or someone sitting in Michigan—to hear about, come and see Luckenbach, with great entertainment. I'm a people watcher. They meet up with friends or total strangers. Luckenbach really is the center of the universe, as Hondo said."

One day an 18-year-old girl from Katy came into the store with her boyfriend. "My mom and dad said I just had to come to Luckenbach," she said. "They used to come here years ago. But I just don't get it!" As she walked further into the store a chicken had just laid an egg on a pile of CDs, and let out a loud squawk and cackle. Abbey picked up the still hot egg and put it into the girl's hands. She shrieked, "Oh my God!" and threw it up in the air. It landed on the floor, didn't even break. Abbey made her welcome even warmer. She comp'd her a Coke and a T-shirt. With her new T-shirt on, grinning from ear to ear, the girl finally admitted, "I get it. This is Luckenbach!"

The Lost Children of Luckenbach (today known as old-timers)

May, 2011

"We are the kids that grew up in Luckenbach in the '70s," one of them said. "Now we are the old ones, some of us already dying off. We are family, not related by blood but melded together by the bonds of hardship, music, and the sharing of our lives. And now, in our more mellow twilight years," said the fortyish-year-old,

MARY LEE EDWARDS

BEER JOINT BABY

MARY LEE EDWARDS

THREE-DOG NIGHT

"we want to remember the hard but good times that brought us all together."

Some of the Luckenbach Regulars, as they were called, still come out today. The roll call would include Roberta Ottmers (Sheriff Marge's daughter), who still weaves hatbands out of beer can tabs. The three Phillips sisters still sing beautiful harmony, twins Valerie and Vickie and sister Dawn. Zip, who slept in his truck, became our One-Man Homeland Security; one riot, one Zip. Stan Easley and son Dillon could be seen playing washers every weekend. John Raven (Bad McFad), now too big to fit in his cannon to be shot off into space, like he was in the '70s, held his own fake wake in the dance hall, just to see if his friends still loved him, and would show up. Old friends came from far and near only to be surprised that he appeared, alive and still kickin'. That's one way to have a reunion. Tell everyone you're dead, then show up for the fun and stories. Some of the Jerry Jeff Walker fans are now scootin' around on their own Jerry Jeff Walkers.

Kimbo Keating, when he took time out from being in trouble, would hypnotize us with his fantastic fiddle. Talented musician Dale Mayfield still comes. And the late Kent Finlay wrote the best ever "Christmastime in Luckenbach" song. Lee McCullough wears suspenders or overalls now. Kathy and Thomas Jacobe and their sons Nicolas and Ian hung out here. The old timer then and now is Wilbur Pehl. Travis Jenske had gorgeous blue eyes. Allegani Jani Schoffield, wife of Tex the Mouth, let the law of gravity babysit her boys, Johnny and Aubrey. Now her grandkids come and play in the mysterious—"is it a cave or is it a dried-up creek bed"– Snail Creek.

Maggie Montgomery, nicknamed the "Songbird of Luckenbach," arrived homeless at Luckenbach from Alabama with her Gibson on her knee. Her address was "Pickup Truck, Texas." It was under those oak trees that her little boy Monte learned to play the guitar in the pickers' circles. Now they call him the "Guitar Wizard," he's compared to Stevie Ray Vaughan, has been on the covers of guitar magazines, and has opened for Bob Dylan.

But the real Luckenbach love story is Tony and Cassey Wilson, of Snail Creek Hat fame. In 1979, teenaged Cassey had a fight with her father and ran away from her home in Adirondack, New York. She ran all the way to Luckenbach after she heard "That Song" on the radio. She followed Waylon's voice and found bartender Tony Wilson, then a drop-dead handsome Montgomery Clift look-alike. She liked his two cute puppies, boots and truck, and that added up to love. They now have a hat shop in the Luckenbach log cabin, Snail Creek Hats.

Those lost, found, or rebellious kids have all grown older, evolved, but still "come home" to Luckenbach. This is how tradition is born. A deeper invisible love is holding us all together under these dusty oak leaf grounds. The tried and true tie that binds us all is, firstly, the music. Secondly, it's the slower, laid back atmosphere that owns us all. Luckenbach is the collection of dear and unique people. They come from France, Houston, Bankersmith, or the Armadillo Farm to slow down, throw off their airs and become Luckenbach heirs.

Jimmy *Lee* Jones: Luckenbach's *Weekday* Bartender/Fire *Marshal*/ Chicken Farmer/*Singer*

September, 2012

Most of Luckenbach's bartenders are also singers. Jimmy Lee Jones has been a permanent fixture in the bar since 1980. He's as regular as the roosters crowing here. Known as Bartender/Fire Marshal, he's also our chief chicken herder, stand-up comic, and

JIMMY LEE JONES, VOICE OF A SINGER AND A MARINE DRILL SARGENT

resident psychologist. Jimmy Lee has been known to hold a crowd spellbound with his music and his jokes for an entire afternoon. As bartender, he'd do tricks and jokes with a wine bottle opener.

"I first came to Luckenbach on leave from the Marines in California, in 1975, for Hondo's Great World's Fair. I knew I had to come back." He did. With his loud, sometimes irreverent ornery voice he often booms at people when they shyly peek in the door. "Y'all want a beer? Don't stand in the doorway, you make the place look shabby!" Or, "If you like me," he'd say, "I'm Jimmy Lee Jones. If you don't, I'm Jerry Jeff Walker."

As resident bar singer he's talented, knows hundreds of songs, and has paid his dues performing in hundreds of festivals, cook-offs, picnics, rodeos and honky-tonks. That booming voice needs no microphone. No wonder, he was a senior drill instructor in the U.S. Marines. It was while stationed in California, he was influenced by a hot local group, "Tall Cotton," and he began to write and sing. His handicap; he had no guitar and he was left-handed. Self-taught, borrowing others' guitars, he'd just flip the guitar over and strum up instead of down.

Drinking a Shiner Bock and holding his upside-down guitar with a cigarette stuck in the capo, he pauses to joke with some older women who have wandered into the bar with their husbands. The part-time Luckenbach bartender has had lots of experience dealing with the tour bus crowd, and he has instantly charmed this group. Possibly hoping to head off his millionth request for "Luckenbach, Texas," he plays Lyle Lovett's "Farther Down the Line." The Luckenbach spirit is in full swing now. "Sheriff" Marge Mueller gives us another round of beers while the tourists alternately gaze at the photos on the wall and huddle around the wood-burning stove.

Jimmy Lee's opened for thirteen of Willie's picnics and shows, even toured with Ray Price in '96 and '97. "I've sung that 'Back to the Basics' Luckenbach song more times than Waylon—maybe twelve times a day."

Likewise, Jimmy Lee changed Luckenbach forever. He and Maggie Montgomery went to Willie's trailer on his golf course in Luck, Texas, and asked him one little question: "Why don't you come sing at Luckenbach?" The rest is history.

Letters *to the* **Moon**

September, 1995
Dear Magnolia,

Remember the tall dirty blonde (or is that dirty tall blonde) you met at Marble Falls through Sandi and Monty? Yep, that's me. I'm loving your Luckenbach Moon *so here's my $15. Send back issues, too and we'll start the script from there. I have Vol. 2 Issue 7.*

June, 2001
To Whom It May Concern:

On Tuesday, May 8, 2001, Luckenbach lost a real friend long before his time. Jeremy Jensen, age 19, was taken from us in a tragic automobile accident on his way to work. Jeremy always looked forward to Luckenbach on any occasion. From the Ladies Chili Cook-off to the Hug-In and Cowboy Caroling around the Campfire, the Fathers of Texas, and the Bluebonnet Ball and even Sunday afternoons on the back porch.

I don't think that anyone can truly understand the importance of a little Hill Country town, until they have heard the stories of Hondo and met the artists and staff and other Luckenbach regulars and visitors, and be treated like people should be treated everywhere. I cannot begin to explain how much Jeremy thought of sitting and talking to Sheriff Marge and Depity James and everyone else that makes up Luckenbach.

I would like to purchase a brick for the patio at the dance hall in Jeremy's memory. Please make the inscription:

In Memory of Jeremy Jenson
1982–2001

To Gary P. Nunn, Rusty Weir, Jerry Jeff Walker, Django Walker, Snuffy Jackson, Ray Wylie Hubbard, Sheriff Marge, Depity James, Mare VelAnne, Jimmy Lee Jones, and all the countless others, thanks for making a difference in a young life. For myself, and the son that I never had, Jeremy Jensen, I cannot begin to express enough thanks for being there.

– Leonard Leinfelder
Waxahachie, Texas

June, 2001

What a wonderful weekend with the most wonderful people in the world, Monte Montgomery and The Montiacs. In the year and a half or so since we had our first encounter with Da Man and the Montiacs, we have had some wonderful times but this beats them all. The Luckenbach show will go down in the annals of history as one of the best ever. Monte was smoking; Lonnie Trevino, Phil Bass and Michael Urdy were on fire along with him. We cannot leave out the beautiful Ms. Jane Clark, the rendition of "When Will I" will never be duplicated. The Montiac Grand Jam before and after the show and the next morning were some of the coolest experiences one could ever imagine.

– Muffin and Bisquit

2011

I just have to tell you that in the '60s, when I was in my early teens, we used to go with Harry and Doris Keller from Fredericksburg to dances. I remember going at night in the middle of nowhere to this place that looked like a barn. I was really frightened but had a great time dancing, as that's my passion. I danced with all ages. When the song "Luckenbach" came out I was more into pop music than country-and-western. I listened though, as being from San Antonio, it was hard to get away from it. It occurred to me once that that was the dark place in the middle of nowhere that I used to go dancing with my parents and their friends. Now that I work at a major airline making reservations, I never book flights to San Antonio without telling the passengers they have to go see Luckenbach.

–Linda Pue

I thought back to my earliest photos in Luckenbach of Guich Koock's son eating peanut butter on crackers and drinking an Orange Crush in the store. And having Hondo drag me and my brother over to the dance hall to watch his little movie he had just made. A private showing. I thought of all the changes our world has gone through, both good and bad and how that little town Hondo helped create has hardly changed at all. Our precious little Earth spins around and around, on its own course, us a captive audience. And we are just people, all in the crazy-scary wonderful world together.

Your friend,
Susan Riley

Editorial *from* Editor Maggie Montgomery
July, 2000

We made it through another July 4th weekend here at Luckenbach. This year nobody nearly died from heat exhaustion. Nobody nearly got busted for doing anything illegal. It didn't take a week to clean up after everybody. Nobody got trampled by the huge crowd. Nobody went home mad.

Compared to the last five years when Willie held his picnic here, it was like a visit to a nice quiet nursing home. And a darn friendly one! A lot of cold beer was consumed. A lot of great music was played and enjoyed. A lot of watermelon, peach ice cream, and hotdogs were consumed. Several Luckenbachians went out into the field where 20,000 people once picnicked and actually stood around and watched the grass grow. We heard Willie liked grass. So we planted some and watered it. You could really see it grow. Other folks took time out to look skyward in search of some sign of rain clouds. None this year.

Remember the last year when Willie came out on the stage and announced that he had a big surprise waiting for everybody at about three o'clock? Sure enough, at three o'clock sharp there was a tremendous rain storm. Nothing like that happened this year.

It looks like we could be faced with what we call a "Luckenbach dilemma." After Willie comes here, we don't have any grass. When he doesn't come, we don't have any rain. It gives us something to ponder while we're waitin' and prayin' for rain, for grass.

Come see us soon.
Maggie Montgomery
Editor in Chief

The Big Littlehorn Battle
Written August, 1965

Cedar Creek would have been a pretty dull town this week if Miguel Schultz, (Pure Indian, Oklahoma, that is) hadn't thought up celebratin' the Big Battle of Littlehorn. We all met at the Park Side Road and had lots to eat. I was with my wash tub on the refreshment committee.

This was the first time Miguel Schultz and Lenny Birmingham Jones (Negro) had spoke to each other after fussin' over whether the Indian or Negro had been mistreated the most.

They shook hands and smoked the piece pipe. (They really don't smoke, I just picked that up on Mr. Joneses TV for a figure of journalism) and Miguel broke out a half pint. They drank it up. Whiskey's a brave maker, and if you're a fighter you'll need an angel and if you're not you'll love the devil. That was explained when Lenny tried to kiss Miguel and he hit him.

That started a argument 'bout The Big Littlehorn Battle. "You guys were worse than we can ever be," said Lenny. "We copied our sit-in-program from your friend Little Bull when he and his tribe sat on the north end of the prairie complainin' about the grassburrs and equal time on gov't horses. When Uncle Sam wouldn't issue thicker pants or divide horse time, it was you guys that took 212 soldiers, 121 horses, one Custer and made a Sioux-flay outa 'em.

Don't you think that Little Bighorn minuette makes a waltz outa Watts?"

"Oh," said Miguel Schultz (Pure Indian).

– Peter Cedarstacker
Writer
Cedar Creek Clippings
1974

Remember: He who laughs lasts —Hondo

The HILL COUNTRY TRAIL of FAME

The region of the German Texas Hill Country is defined by a chain of hills that form a divide between the Guadalupe and Pedernales Rivers. Nestled among the backbone of these hills is a visible—or not so visible—string of little German "towns."

During the 1840s and 1850s, these little towns had had a remarkable and unique impact on Texas, the nation, and the world as a whole. Sisterdale, Luckenbach and Grapetown, only 10 minutes apart, might be mistaken for ghost towns at first glance, each marked by only two or three weathered buildings with a county road running through them. A passerby might never notice them at all. But what endures, however, are the ideals that formed the backbones of these communities.

Their inhabitants were revolutionaries. Their intellects and ideals were ahead of their times, aflame with imagination and ideas for new inventions. As immigrants, they had courage, a tough spirit that enabled them to survive the frontier miseries, tragedies and hardships that befell them. They all had heirs that disappeared too young; they fought wars against Anglos, Indians and ingrained regional prejudice with the nonviolent weapons of peace, education, music, literature and utopian ideals for basic human rights.

They were botanists and geologists, who observed and wrote about the world around them. They were farmers who plowed the ground, literally and intellectually. You can't really understand Luckenbach, and what makes it special, without delving into the history, culture and the people who made the region what it is. Not all of the story is pretty, but it's indispensable. The German Texas Hill Country was then, and still is, in my mind's eye, the center of the universe.

THE TREATY

Baron von Meusebach, *Peacemaker*

"Tenax propositi", ("Tenacity of purpose")

—Meusebach's family motto

The largest national group to immigrate from Europe to America was the Germans, from 1845–1861, and most of them came to Texas. In those years, they left Germany because of over-population. The lack of organization or jobs made life exceedingly difficult. Lower classes needed to leave Germany or die; things were that bad.

Also, there was a calculated campaign to encourage emigration that created among some Germans a wanderlust for the Texas frontier. The first group, some 7,400, arrived in 1845, (most of them entering at the Texas ports of Galveston and Indianola) and traveled to Fredericksburg and New Braunfels. They were mainly craftsmen, tradesmen and wine and beer makers.

A young Texas frontier would not have developed, nor would the Central Texas German towns exist, had it not been for the remarkable peace treaty that was struck between the German settlers and the Native Americans. On the banks of the San Saba River in the Hill Country around

Fredericksburg, an agreement was made by Baron Johan Von Meusebach and the chiefs of the fierce Penateka-Comanche tribe. It would eventually open up four million acres for peaceful white settlement and create ten Texas counties.

Meusebach, a wealthy, highly educated judge from Germany, emigrated to Texas in1845. At 32, he took over the failed immigration fiasco of Prince Carl of Solms Braunfels and became head of the German Immigration Society of Texas. Meusebach had the daunting task of preparing a place for 4,000 immigrants who'd arrived from the Gulf of Mexico by walking 250 miles inland. Due to Prince Solms' financial debts, they had none of the wagons (most were being used for the Mexican American War of 1845), money or supplies that had been promised. Two thousand perished on the walk from disease, exhaustion and exposure.

In 1846, the first thing Meusebach did was to found the town of Fredericksburg. The disreputable Henry Fischer, who held title to much of the area, knew the land was infested with Comanches but didn't tell the Germans. The resulting Fischer-Miller Grant between the Republic of Texas and the newcomers allowed thousands of colonists to settle in the heart of Indian hunting grounds, but did not allow them to own land. Inheriting Solms' $40,000 debt, Meusebach had $20,000 of his own money with which he bought 125 acres from a Mexico City native for the new citizens of Fredericksburg. Forty-six huts were built, a town hall, and the *Vereins Kirche* ("One Church For All") were erected.

In 1847, a year later, he was determined to explore the uncharted Indian territory north of the Llano River and create a friendly relationship with the ferocious and combative Comanches before any trouble could start. He had a deadline, August 1847, or the land grant would be forfeited by the Republic of Texas. And worse, 4,000 more immigrants were coming in November, 1847.

In late January, Meusebach started on one of the most remarkable journeys ever undertaken by a white man in Texas. He left Fredericksburg with three wagons and 40 men. Riding for days, he saw no Indians, but he knew they were watching him. By February 5, near what is now the town of Mason, a vanguard consisting of a minor Comanche chief, Ketsumsee, and eight warriors approached the party on foot, carrying a white flag, wanting to know their purpose. There were also 500 painted warriors on horseback accompanying the smaller group.

Meusebach dismounted, leaving his gun in the saddle. Even though he was vastly outnumbered he bravely said, "We've come to talk peace, or we can fight. My men are well-armed and there will be much wailing in the Comanche camp." Meusebach said he wanted a general conference with all the other Comanche chiefs to be held further north on the San Saba River. They shared a meal. On February 6, they led Meusebach to their camp.

Meusebach reduced his men to 17, sent the wagons back home, and journeyed on to the San Saba. In his group was interpreter Lorenzo de Rojas (who had been kidnapped by Comanches), the Indian agent Army Sgt. Neighbors, interpreter Jim Shaw, some Delaware and Shawnee Indians to scout and hunt, five Germans and some Mexican muleteers. Also in the group was botanist Ferdinand von Roemer, sent to Texas by the Berlin Academy of Science to evaluate the mineral assets of the land grant.

When they crossed the San Saba, you can imagine how the small group felt when they came upon two miles of white teepees, 1,000 horses, thousands of painted warriors on horseback, and hundreds of women, children, and prisoners in one vast group. Meusebach made a memorable first impression of his own; At six-foot-two inches, with red hair, he was a formidable figure. Texas Ranger Jack Hays had advised him it would impress the Indians further if he rode a white horse. He did, and it did.

Meusebach spurred his horse to a trot and bravely fired his rifle in the air to empty his weapon, as did his men. This risky but smart move earned the Indians' trust. The Indians moved like a slow lava flow towards them. While staying in the Comanche camp waiting for the other chiefs to arrive, von Roemer noted Meusebach's courage walking among the Comanches unarmed, a habit that further increased the Indians' respect for the Germans.

On March 1, 1847, the terms of the treaty were discussed. The meeting was held with 20 chiefs sitting on buffalo skins. The three main chiefs were Buffalo Hump, Santa Anna, and Old Owl. The peace pipe was passed around twice in silence between the chiefs and Meusebach and his entourage at the tent village on the San Saba. Gifts had been presented to the Indians: wool saddle blankets, cloth, copper wire for bracelets, salt and corn. More gifts and money in the value of $3,000 were promised later, if and when the treaty was signed.

More important than the objects traded were the words and terms of equality, dignity and recognition. Meusebach spoke his terms clearly after the pipe ceremony: that his people would be permitted to come and go, build their communities, and the Comanches would in turn promise not to disturb the surveyors or colonists.

> *"You are to be treated with fairness, and welcome to our homes and towns. We do not look at you as inferior," Meusebach continued, "nor are we superior. We do not want to drive the Comanches from their land. We hope to live together as brothers even though we are different. Later, we will welcome your young to marry with our young."*

He also stressed that his people were neither Texan or Mexican, the two groups hated most by Comanches. The Indians were impressed by his humility, bravery, his white horse and red hair, and the fact that he didn't wear a uniform. They named him *Sol*

Colorado (Red Sun) and Chief Burning Hair. Meusebach dropped the "Baron" from his name and from then on was simply just called "John" by everyone.

The Comanche chiefs told the Germans to give them two moons (months) to decide, but that they could not promise the cooperation of the Comanches further away. This would only be a treaty between the private citizens of the Fischer-Miller Grant and the Penateka-Comanche tribe.

In the spring of 1847, thousands of Indians started moving toward Fredericksburg. The Indians, still untrusting, remembered the killing of many of their chiefs in ambush when they assembled at Council House in San Antonio in 1838. In 1840, Buffalo Hump sought revenge for the Council House fight by attacking Victoria, Texas with 600 warriors and destroying the town of Linnville. Peace with the whites seemed unthinkable.

Therefore, the Comanches lit signal fires on the surrounding hills of Fredericksburg and if one was snuffed out it would be a signal for trouble. Mothers in their little log cabins calmed their frightened children by making up stories. "Those are Easter fires. The Easter rabbit is dyeing the eggs with wildflowers in large pots." Satisfied with this wild tale, they could then sleep. Easter fires are still lit today on the surrounding hills of Fredericksburg each Easter Eve.

In Fredericksburg, on May 9, 1847, the chiefs signed the treaty with their marks. Gifts were exchanged. The Indians brought 67 deerskins, honey, and 56 bags of bear fat (there were a lot of bears back then). There was dancing and chanting, with the Indians using the Germans' big wooden cheese boxes as drums.

A great gesture was then made by the Lipan Apache Indians—to free stolen Comanche horses (marked with a slit ear). Forty were given to Fort Martin Scott in Fredericksburg. In general, no horses were stolen by Indians in Comal and Gillespie Counties again. And this at a time when Comanches and Apaches were slaughtering white settlers from the Texas Panhandle to the Mexican border.

Let's remember the honesty, humility and bravery of unprejudiced John Meusebach, and the peace that those Easter fires brought. The Meusebach-Comanche Treaty was the only known peace treaty with Native American Indians in U.S. history never to be broken.

"The Freethinkers" *and* The Civil War

The second large group that immigrated from Germany in 1850, a massive influx of 20,000, which included my ancestors, was very different from the first arrivals in 1845. Known as the "Freethinkers," they were made up of aristocrats, doctors, philosophers, professors, poets, writers and intellectuals. They had escaped Germany, where they were being persecuted, imprisoned and tortured, simply for having new ideas.

For Germans arriving in Texas in the mid-1850s, a whole new set of conflicts presented themselves. There were the Indian and slave problems, yes—but the Anglos would do more harm to the Germans than would anyone else. To understand the ideals of the German "Freethinkers" is to understand the trouble and danger they were confronted with at that time in history.

The Freethinkers' large utopian democratic society took up most of the Hill Country. Upon arrival, they promptly established strings of little communities like Bettina, Castell, Cypress

Mill, Sisterdale, Boerne (then called Tuluscum), Kerrville, and Luckenbach (then called Grape Creek). Some grew and thrived. Some didn't.

Their citizens advocated reason over religious and political authoritarianism and valued their freedom of speech. They were anti-slavery abolitionists who rejected secession during the Civil War, even as the rest of Texas joined the Confederacy.

They had their own separate rules: welcoming runaway slaves, Mexicans, and Indians; advocating education for women and all races; a general disregard for religious dogma.

No churches were allowed in their communities, since the Freethinkers were against organized religion. Comfort finally got a church fifty years after it was settled, because the train wouldn't stop in a town without one. No lawyers were allowed to live in the town because they attracted problems, were peace-breakers.

The Germans' religion was culture. They brought books, paintings and musical instruments to an untutored and intellectually barren frontier. Known as the "Latin Colony," the Freethinkers conducted meetings in Latin, especially those in Sisterdale. Everyone was harmonious, cheerful, easygoing, *gemütlich*—that last word coming from *Gemütlichkeit*, which means "comfort" or "coziness." The term is most commonly associated with the easygoing tenor of a German beer garden. The Germans worked, played, and organized hard. Their social activities—the reading, shooting, singing, and exercise clubs—eventually formed the center of their Unionist, anti-slavery movement.

It was at a state singing festival in San Antonio that they first began to talk of revolution against the Confederacy. In June of 1861, Sisterdale's Edward Degener formed a loyal Union League (*Freier Verein*), or Free Club, that pledged to remain "true to the Union," and swear loyalty to their first government, the United States. At the 1854 Singing Fest, they adopted a political and religious platform including abolition of capital punishment, abolition of slavery, total separation of church from state, and equal pay for equal work. In doing so, they made themselves targets for the political, military and social powers-that-be at the time.

In 1861, Texas secession erupted into war. The Germans thought they could quietly stick to their ideals of freedom of speech, ignore the war, be treated as conscientious objectors and ride out the conflict. This was dangerously naïve on their part. The Unionists and abolitionists were immediately considered spies and traitors by the new Confederate government in Austin.

"The *Hangebund*," or "Hanging Gang"

Since the Texas Hill Country was far removed from the main battlefields of the Civil War, no immediate cause for alarm existed among the Freethinkers. However, when it became known that many of the Germans didn't sympathize with slavery, secession, or the Confederacy, martial law was declared. James P. Waldrip and his *Hangebund* ("hanging band") mob and Captain James Duff, who precipitated the Nueces Massacre in 1862 were two of the worst of those who abused their powers and incited fear among the German population in the Hill Country.

In 1861, a light vote in Kerr County showed most citizens were against secession (34 for, 53 against). Even deposed Governor Sam Houston gave a speech explaining the dangers of secession. No matter. The communities of Bear Creek, Luckenbach, Sisterdale,

Grapetown, and Fredericksburg were terrorized by the self-proclaimed vigilante Waldrip during the *Henkerzeiten* ("Hanging times") in 1862.

Just like the Missouri-based terrorist William Quantrill, James P. Waldrip and his hanging gang struck fear and dread into the innocent families they victimized. Waldrip always called the men out of their homes at night to hang them, so neighbors at Luckenbach area lit lamps to warn others that the *Hangebund* was passing by.

A *Hangebund* of twenty men went on a killing spree in Luckenbach (Grape Creek) on March 9, 1864, killing five innocent German ranchers in one day. Clara Feller tried to pass a gun under her apron to her husband Bill but failed. Here is her testimony:

"...one of the men leaped forward and tore the gun from my hand... more came in... they grabbed the other two guns. They were rough! They took our saddle outfit, our horse, and Bill. Then two shots fell some distance away... they would not let me go along with my husband. Oh, God, that night of horror I shall never forget! My seven children were all crying. The oldest was twelve."

Luckenbach's Peter Berg was shot in front of his house. Three, Bill Feller, Mr. Blank and Mr. Kirchner, were hung in one tree until they died of suffocation.

In Pecan Creek, a father hid for two years in a hole in his pasture camouflaged by a green bush. "Bushwhacker", became a new term, as the renegades "knocked" on every bush. Mr. Peter Bonn crept back into Fredericksburg at night, dressed in his wife's dress and bonnet to work in the fields during the day. Mr. Conrad Wehmeyer, an outspoken Unionist, hid in the attic of his bakery. The men had to be creative to stay alive. Bottom line: every German was suspect. The vigilantes continued to terrorize the Hill Country with impunity. Thousands fled.

Battle *of the* Nueces

Everyone's heard of the battles of Shiloh, Gettysburg, Vicksburg and Bull Run that helped define the War Between the States. Relatively few have heard of the Battle of the Nueces in Texas. But to the freethinking German citizens of the Hill Country, that local conflict was as impactful as any Civil War battle in the history books. In April of 1862, the Conscript Act required Confederate military service of all males over age sixteen, beginning with registering for the draft. Part of the purpose of the Act was to identify all disloyal persons who might be disinclined to register and swear allegiance to the Confederacy.

The Hill Country Germans never accepted this new reality. Their intellectual attitude made them adamantly and dangerously independent. The malicious Scottish-born Capt. James Duff (known as the "Butcher of Fredericksburg") and his Partisan Rangers were appointed by Governor Ed Clark to oversee martial law in the Hill Country and to demand Confederate loyalty oaths. Many Germans refused to take one, even when threatened. Families were divided.

The new governor issued a proclamation allowing all those who wouldn't pledge allegiance be allowed to peacefully leave the state in 30 days. Sixty-four young German men (none over 35) from Comal, Kerr, Kendall and Gillespie Counties met August 1, 1862 at Turtle Creek, near Kerrville, determined to leave Texas by way of Mexico, and thereupon return and join the Union Army. Among this group were Sisterdale's Hugo (age 20) and Hilmer (age 21) Degener, sons of Edward, a prominent Sisterdale settler and future U.S. Congressman. In addition, there was Turtle Creek's Emil Schreiner (an ancestor of mine), August Luckenbach, brother of original settler Jacob Luckenbach (and whose son, Albert, was the town's namesake) and Comfort's Heinrich Stieler (age 16), the youngest, my great-grand uncle. There were also five Americans and one Mexican citizen, Pablo Diaz.

Most were equipped with old muzzle-loading German-made rifles and six-shooters. Some had no guns at all. Some had only musical instruments. Since these men were leaving peacefully and lawfully, according to the terms the governor had set forth, they had no fear of being followed by Duff, who nonetheless called their exodus a rebellion and set out in pursuit with his band of Rangers.

A traitor named Bergman led Duff to the spot where the Germans were camped along the Nueces River, twenty-five miles from Fort Clark and fifty miles from the Rio Grande and the Mexican border.

On August 10, at four in the morning, Duff's men, one hundred strong, attacked. The Germans fought valiantly for one hour. Nineteen were killed. Some fled between attacks. Duff's men executed nine wounded Germans in cold blood, with shots to the back of their heads. My 16-year-old great grand-uncle, Heinrich Stieler, and his 18-year-old friend fled but were later tracked down and hung, at Goat Creek near Kerrville, their bodies disemboweled, with "spy" signs around their necks. Eight were killed three months later crossing the Rio Grande. Eleven survived to join the Union Army—some walking 900 miles to Monterey, then to Vera Cruz, sailing to New Orleans.

The "Luckenbach Bushwhackers"

A "Bushwhacker" could be either a Union or Confederate sympathizer; "bush", meaning a surprise attack, or hiding in the cedar breaks from vigilantes. Both sides used this situation for personal benefit, to settle old arguments, feuds, or as retaliation, carried out under the guise of military orders. This war-within-a-war was in full force during the summer of 1862.

Captain *James Duff*'s Partisan Ranger Company of murderers were notorious anti-Union vigilantes (as seen at the Nueces Massacre). But there was another guerilla group known as the "Luckenbach Bushwhackers," members of the Hill Country Militia who targeted Confederate sympathizers with destruction.

Their rebellion would be in the form of draft dodging, refusing Confederate currency, resorting to verbal and physical abuse, and maintaining a spy system for the Unionists of the North. The "Luckenbach Bushwhackers," became more engaged in severe and escalating reprisals, like the burning of barns and property, even though they knew they risked severe atrocities against them and their families, destruction or confiscation of their property or possible death in return.

The "Luckenbach Bushwhackers" leaders were especially sought after by the Confederates. *August Luckenbach*, age 28, the leader of the group, who had been at the Nueces Massacre on August 10th, but who had escaped, was captured ten days later and hanged. *Conrad Bock*, age 26, was also a member of the "Luckenbach Bushwhackers." He was captured and hung north of Boerne near Cibolo Creek on August 23rd.

There were other "Luckenbach Bushwhackers" who were murdered on a second attempt to flee to Mexico three months later: *John George Kallenburg* (William Luckenbach's brother-in-law), *Adolph* (22) and brother *Louis* (19) *Ruebsamen. Jacob Kusenberger* (28) survived the Nueces Massacre but didn't attempt to come home. He made it to the Rio Grande, three days without food and water, swam across, caught a ship at Matamoros, sailed to New Orleans, and enlisted in the Union Army.

"Luckenbach Bushwhacker" *Frank Weiss* (19) was shot in the water at the Rio Grande. His older brother *Moritz Weiss* (26) drowned while trying to help his wounded brother cross the river. While at the Rio Grande, "Luckenbach Bushwhacker" *Sylvester Kleck* (17), received several gunshot wounds and grabbed the tail of a horse that dragged him to the Mexican side. He was nursed back to health at Piedras Negras by *Juanita* (15). They later married.

Eight were killed. All were young.

The viciousness against the Union sympathizers reached epidemic proportions. The hunt for "Dutchmen" and others continued into many Texas counties beyond the Hill Country. Hundreds had been lynched without a trial. Their officers brushed off these atrocities explaining that they "meant well." The Union sympathizers died for their beliefs.

After the Civil War, a Kendall County Reconstruction Jury indicted Captain *James Duff* and slated him for execution, but he was never found or tried.

Three years later, in 1865 after the war's conclusion, the bones of the massacred victims were recovered. Thirty-five of their names are on a *Treue Der Union* ("True to the Union") monument in Comfort, Texas, where the bones were interred. One of those names is my great-great uncle, 16 year-old Heinrich Stieler, "captured and murdered." It is the only Union monument on Southern soil marking the names of unmustered loyalists. The monument is one of only six in the U.S. allowed to fly its flag at half-mast perpetually.

Luckenbach, Sisterdale and Comfort didn't grow for years because of the great loss of their young men. The only fault of these citizens was that they were too idealistic. Edward Degener, of Sisterdale, who had lofty ideas about American liberty, imparted these convictions to his sons, two of whom were killed at the Nueces and another of whom was imprisoned. He said that although his sons lacked a good education in this new land, above all he wanted to teach them to work for their own sustenance and to have "minds free from prejudice, and spirits which would sustain their individual conclusions without a thought of consequences." But there would be no more attempts by the Freethinkers for a cooperative or a perfect utopian community.

Sophisticated Sisterdale

Sisterdale, located in the valley of Sister Creek, a few miles south of Luckenbach on FM 1376, was home to a sophisticated circle of intellectuals. Nicholas Zink, a German engineer, who had already built roads in Greece, founded Sisterdale in 1847.

Frederick Law Olmstead, a botanist and landscape architect, wandered through the area and wrote about Sisterdale in 1857 in one of his most famous travel books, *A Journey Through Texas*. Olmstead is best known today for designing New York's magnificent Central Park. Another member of this illustrious circle, Ottmar von Behr, a meteorologist and naturalist, named Sisterdale. Sisterdale was the central community for the Freethinkers. The prestigious circle included Baron von Westphal (a brother-in-law of Karl Marx). The leader of these farmers was Dr. Ernst Kapp, a Freethinker who had been prosecuted for sedition in the 1840s, was exiled from Germany for publishing a controversial article about despotism, ahead of its time. The article was called *Der konstituiert Despotismus und die konstitutionelle Freiheit*, 1849 (The Constitutional Despotism and the Constitutional Freedom). A geologist and philosopher, he became President of the Freethinker Abolitionist Organization headquartered in Sisterdale.

Dr. Kapp wrote a book that was important enough to be distributed throughout Germany, *Principles of the Philosophy of Technology* (1877), which contained ideas dating back to the time of Aristotle. It analyzed the language and the state as extensions of mental life, long before such ideas were popularized. Dr. Kapp operated a spa in Sisterdale called *Badenthal*, which offered water-cures for ailments and gym exercises for health.

While things have changed in this 21st century, Central Texans still share many of the characteristics of the Freethinkers who helped settle the Hill Country; the communities are unincorporated, their attitude being less government, the better. The citizens celebrate individualism, and as such, they are conservative, hard-working, confident, friendly, and patriotic.

The faded history of Luckenbach still bleeds through to today. Luckenbach, as one of the Civil War Unionist German-Texas communities in a Southern state, has roots that go deep. Those roots manifest themselves today in a present-day philosophy, that values an independent spirit and the celebration of personal freedoms. *Gemütlichkeit* (meaning comfort), and equality for all races and egos, where everybody's treated like somebody, is Luckenbach's proud German legacy today.

JACOB BRODBECK

Luckenbach's *Inventor*, *Educator*, Musician

Not many people know that one of Luckenbach's most prestigious heroes is Jacob Brodbeck. Arriving in Luckenbach from Fredericksburg in 1858, Brodbeck was one of Gillespie County's and Luckenbach's first teachers, a mechanical genius, musician and inventor. His invention? A flying machine which lifted off a whopping 40 years before the Wright brothers, and before the invention of any gas-powered engine.

In 1839, as an 18-year-old immigrant, while sailing from Germany to the Texas port of Indianola, ideas were already coming to him: He watched the wings of the gulls, studied the angles of the sails, and the air currents that moved the ship. Thus, he thought of building an "airship," using the atmosphere instead of battling waves for transportation. He mentioned his dream to Baron von Meusebach, Fredericksburg's founder and peace-keeper with the Comanches. Meusebach encouraged his dream but gave him practical employment as Fredericksburg's second teacher at the *Vereins Kirche* from 1847–1849 in Fredericksburg.

Brodbeck married Christina Beherens, who was only 13 at the time. He was 37 years old, 24 years her senior. In 1858, they moved to Luckenbach, (then called Grape Creek) into an existing log house. In 1860, Jacob taught at Luckenbach's first school, which was called Grape Hill. Brodbeck became the County Surveyor after the previous one was killed by Indians in 1862, but he resigned after a year because he wanted more time to develop his airship idea.

By 1863, he wanted to journey to San Antonio to build a larger model that would hold an "aeronaut". This venture took him away from his family for over six years. One can only imagine what his wife Christina, herself still a teenager, thought of his obsession and prolonged absence.

In San Antonio, he would teach piano and tune pianos. His brother Georg looked after Jacob's family for all this time. Jacob Brodbeck struck up a friendship with San Antonio doctor named Ferdinand Herff, that would last a lifetime. (Herff, also a German immigrant and Freethinker, was the first doctor to use ether for surgery in Texas). Herff gave Brodbeck financial and moral support and helped him go public in 1865 by selling stock at $5.00 a share.

Herff wrote to potential investors, "... as Texas inventions are novelties in the world of art and science, we hasten to lay the call before our readers and the world at large... to enable man to use, like a bird, the atmosphere region as a medium of his travels." Dr. Herff as well as Mr. August Engel who lived at Luckenbach at that time, both bought shares.

He called it a ship because it was constructed like one. The "hull" held one aeronaut, the power plant, and the steering mechanism. It was enclosed to prevent "rapid motion from affecting breathing." In the bow, there was a propeller screw for navigating in water (if it landed in any nearby ocean, lake, river, or stock tank). The upper portion consisted of horizontal sails,

LUCKENBACH ARCHIVES

JACOB BRODBECK PORTRAIT

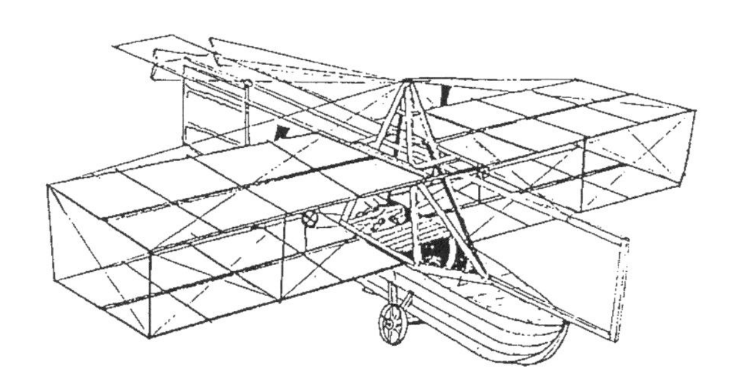

JACOB BRODBECK'S 1862 AIRSHIP AND SIGNATURE.
(DRAWING BY FERNANDO CORTEZ OF SAN ANTONIO)

partly immovable, partly movable. The third portion produced the forward motion, consisting of two screws for lateral steering. The pilot would have a crank in each hand—one to guide ascent and descent, the other for lateral steering. There was also a compass and barometer and a speed gauge (similar to a ball regulator on a steam engine). The speed depended on motive power (a wind-up coil) and wind direction. He estimated he could attain speeds at 30 to 100 mph.

By June, 1865, Brodbeck had enough money to build a larger model and his shareholders were getting anxious to see something! At Dr. Ferdinand Herff's ranch in Boerne, he demonstrated his first big flight. Neighbors helped build a 20-foot platform onto which they hoisted the "ship" for extra take-off lift.

Brodbeck himself described the maiden voyage: "A rather large crowd gathered to watch the unusual affair. There were many military men there, plus my dear friend from Fredericksburg, Charles H. Nimitz, who gave a speech in my honor". Immigrant Nimitz was a former seaman and grandfather of the famous Admiral Chester W. Nimitz, Commander-in-Chief of the Pacific Fleet in World War II.

"Nimitz had tried to convince the government that my 'Air Ship' would be a great asset to the military," Brodbeck continued. "Nimitz had been a border officer of the Confederate Army during the Civil War... I said a few prayers as I crawled into the aeronaut's chamber. I wound up the massive coil spring and cut loose the rope as I released the lever for the take-off. The take-off was a success and the 'Air Ship' soared majestically over the treetops. As the coil spring unwound, suddenly something happened with the mechanism and I was unable to rewind the spring fast enough to remain aloft. I found myself dashing toward the ground with my spirit shattered. I suffered only minor injuries, but my pride and joy suffered severe damage."

The craft was stored in Herff's barn in the town of Boerne until Brodbeck had enough money to rebuild again. He never could figure out how to rewind an unwinding coil for motive power even though he'd invented a self-winding clock for the King of Germany. Sadly, Brodbeck received criticism for his "crazy" ideas and for leaving his family for such a long period, plus he still felt forlorn about the crash of his dream ship. Jacob and his brother Georg took a flatbed wagon to Boerne to transport the ruins of his airship to his Luckenbach farm.

Having been gone from his Luckenbach family for over six years, he wanted to return to continue working on his ship. After finishing his term as School Inspector for Bexar County he went home to Luckenbach. Jacob and Christina acquired more land at Luckenbach. They were able to purchase a 320-acre tract being sold for back taxes for $6.00! They also bought 500 acres at 50 cents an acre.

In 1874, there was an account of a Luckenbach "flight." The grand- daughter of Henry Habenicht told how her grandfather was one of the neighbors who helped hoist the airship on the roof to take off.

He recounted the historic event thusly: "It took off in a straight line gaining a miraculous 12 feet above ground and traveled 100 feet before it crashed into Georg's cornfield and into a chicken coop."

In Brodbeck's own words: "I looked forward to flying like a bird again. My ship took off and I sailed around until the power of the coil spring gave out again after a few minutes of flight. Then down into the cornfield I crashed but I was not badly injured, only bruised from head to toe. I know some of my neighbors felt sorry for me but yet others called me a *crazy old man.*"

Jacob became aware of Octave Chanute and his glider experiments; Chanute flew gliders off of 95-foot high sand dunes at Dune

Park near Lake Michigan. They arranged to meet in Michigan when Brodbeck was visiting a nephew in the vicinity.

Chanute asked Brodbeck many questions and saw his small model. Chanute eventually built a biplane similar to Brodbeck's construction and was finally successful with a steady flight. With no luck in securing investors thus far, Brodbeck demonstrated his model to many businessmen in Michigan, all of whom were unwilling to back him. Jacob then went to Chicago to demonstrate the model and while there, some important papers were stolen from his briefcase. Jacob always felt that his plans were used to help those who were later successful in achieving flight due to the invention of the small gasoline motor. Again, he returned to Luckenbach with a weary heart to a family who barely recognized him because of his rag-tag appearance. They had not heard if he was alive or dead.

In the 1870s, Brodbeck was Gillespie County's Commissioner for two years. He was also very active in building the Luckenbach school (called Grape Hill, District 8) in 1844, and became one of its first teachers. In 1886, at age 65, his last son of ten was born. His life took on a more conventional appearance, but he still harbored his elusive vision of powered flight.

In spite of his absences, he took time to teach his kids music. His very talented son, Hilmar, played the organ and was the music director for the Luckenbach choral group "Frohsinn." Another son, Arthur, was also artistic, inventive, and a music composer. Arthur played in the Luckenbach brass band.

As most know today, the Texas Hill Country has become akin to a little Napa Valley, with its abundance of vineyards, wineries and tasting venues, especially on the stretch of Highway 290 that flies by Luckenbach. The German immigrants, like Fredericks-burg's founder John Meusebach and Brodbeck, could've predicted this. They had brought with them from Germany vine cuttings that combined the heart of sweetness and root of hardiness. The plants thrived in the thin Hill Country soil.

Brodbeck, always without money, sold his own wine to raise funds to pursue his dream. With the profits from wine sales and investments from investors, he was able to continue building on his air ship. Brodbeck's wine gained popularity throughout Gillespie County. He sold it to his friends, strangers, and even taverns for mainstream distribution.

In 1894, there was an account from Richard Brehmer (Sheriff Marge's grandfather), who at age seven, had witnessed perhaps the last flight attempt by Brodbeck in Luckenbach; proof that at age 73 he was still trying to improve his invention. Brehmer stated that Jacob said in German, "*Buben, ich will mahl seben ob mein bogel jetz fleight.*" ("Children, I want to see if my bird will fly now.") Alas, his effort came to naught.

At 76, Jacob finally gave up a 30-year struggle to develop a better method of motive power for an aircraft. In 1904, he heard that an aircraft had been developed and flown by a pair of brothers named Wilbur and Orville Wright who owned a bicycle shop in Ohio. He was not surprised. He felt his ideas and plans had somehow gotten into their hands.

In 1968, Henderson Shuffer, in researching for San Antonio's Hemisfair World's Fair, found a story that the Wright brothers constructed a crude structure from an old negative found in a Dayton, Ohio building which was being demolished. Could it have been a picture of Jacob's machine?

Jacob Brodbeck died six years later in 1910 at age 89. He was buried at his Luckenbach farm, marked by a granite headstone. Brodbeck's ideas were ahead of their time. He *did* conquer gravity, and he did have something to do with the goal of manned flight, even if that achievement was realized by someone else. Furthermore, he was a success as a great educator and inspiration for students and future leaders. And his sons were Luckenbach's first pioneer Texas musicians. In 1967, then-Gov. John Connally proclaimed Brodbeck "The Father of Aviation." Half a century later, a Texas historical marker was dedicated to him and placed on his farm at Luckenbach in 2018. Something tells me that he and Hondo would have gotten along swimmingly.

FESTS

Life was exceedingly hard on the Texas frontier and it grew not much less fraught and difficult even after the Indian wars subsided and the Civil War was concluded. The farms and small towns of the Texas Hill Country were isolated in a way that is hard to envision today. (For a vivid picture of the hardscrabble way of life in the region in the pre-New Deal days, I can recommend the chapter "The Sad Irons" from *The Path to Power* [1982], author Robert Caro's first volume of his massive biography of Lyndon B. Johnson.)

Cut off from the rest of the world by the flood-prone rivers and ridges of spiny, rocky hills, the denizens of towns like Grapetown, Kendalia, Sisterdale and Luckenbach had to manufacture their own entertainment. Traditional German festivals, imported to Texas from the old country, were one way of easing the isolation.

Grapetown *and* Luckenbach: Singing *and* Shooting Fests

In Germany, every town had a choir, a shooting club, and a theatre association. Customs like the *Schuetzenfest* (the shooting festival) and *Saengerfest* (singing societies' musical festival) were the patriotic glue that held these little communities and their German culture together.

Another little ghost town down the road, like Luckenbach and Sisterdale, is Grapetown on South Grape Creek Road (or 7325 Old San Antonio Road). The drive down Grape Creek Road is bucolic and pastoral, with sheep in deep green oat fields, laboriously built winding rock fences and wonderful still-standing 19th century houses, smokehouses and barns, all made of field stone. You might drive right past Grapetown if you don't know what to look for. Grapetown's only four buildings represented what was important to the Freethinkers; a schoolhouse, a smokehouse (for curing sausage), a dance hall, and a shooting range.

Like the others, it was started in 1848 as a Freethinker unincorporated farming and ranching community. Here too, they were affected by the Nueces Massacre.

In 1887, Grapetown combined the singing and shooting clubs together with those in Luckenbach and in 1895 became the host to the first annual Gillespie County "Marksman Festival." In the Luckenbach bar, there's a photo of the 1888 Grapetown S*chuetzen Verein*. Still active today, the event always includes crowning of a *Schuetzen Koenig* (King of the Marksmen), a parade with each groups' club flags and a *Saengerfest*.

The *Schuetzen Bund* shoot very long target rifles—six feet from stock to muzzle. The .22 rim-fire is known as the "Little King." The .22-250 is the slightly bigger caliber, or "Big King." Both have extension barrels screwed on for more accuracy over a long distance.

Gary Frantzen and Charles Worrell of Fredericksburg are two gunsmiths who still craft these unusual and rare guns today.

Shooting clubs are still active today in Bear Creek, Tivydale, Barons Creek, Hubertes, Scharf, and Grapetown. The shooters prop their long rifles on wooden rests and shoot 200 yards. There are ten brave people down in the six-foot deep trench changing the target after each shot.

The *Schuetzenfests* were big outings and an excuse for the whole family to camp out. The women worked hard preparing food while the men shot the bull as well as at the targets. Typical of the practical Germans, usually money was raised for the hiring of a school teacher for the one-room school or for the benefit of the club itself. Barbeque was sold to the public, as well as homemade butter and baked goods.

The evening's entertainment was usually a dance. The S*chuetzen Koenig* who was the high-point scorer, was awarded a medal and carried around on the shoulders of admirers. But the lesser winners got to choose, in order of rank, from among a more practical array of prizes. First to go were bullets and motor oil. Next was the Purina Dog Chow, aluminum chairs, calico sacks of flour, chicken feed and knives. Last chosen was the one towel and matching washcloth with matching handmade artwork. There was the goat shoot-off; the goat being the prize not the target.

You can usually find a practice shoot going on at Bear Creek Community the first Sunday of every month. Tradition dictates that the big *Schuetzenfest* Championship is always held on a full moon

LUCKENBACH ARCHIVES

GRAPE TOWN SHOOTING CLUB
1888

LUCKENBACH ARCHIVES

LUCKENBACH'S FROHSINN MEN'S CHOIR
1888

date. A full moon was preferred, so the horses could see better at night returning home.

The names, as well as the guns, are handed down over generations. Some of the original members' names are still active today: Old World families like Feller, Schmidt, Basse, Flach, Herbort, and Staudt. One year Zeo Weinheimer of Fredericksburg was the Little *Schuetzen Koenig* for the biggest Little *Schuetzenfest* in Gillespie County, when 73 sharpshooters participated. He was the Big Shot of the Little Shot.

In addition to shooting, there is singing. The *Saengerfests* still keep our hills alive with the sound of traditional German music. (Julie Andrews would feel right at home).

If you ever sit in the presence of the glorious sound of German choirs around the Hill Country, your heart will swell with beauty and pride to be in the presence of this historic, well-loved tradition. Arising from the tradition carried over from Germany to Texas, these singing clubs were driven by the pure love of singing in groups.

Luckenbach, always a seat of culture, had a singing club, the Frohsinn Men's Choir, that was formed in 1884.

The two main clubs today in Fredericksburg are *Arion Maennechor* (for men only) and *Hermannsohne Gemister Chor* (a co-ed society), founded in 1934. Ever since that year, the beloved old song "Lorelei" is always the first to be performed. Dues in the '30s were ten cents a month. The choir bought a dollar's worth of wood to heat the hall for winter months. And when a flag was appointed to be made, a Mr. Felix Hahne *loaned* the choir money for the flag.

During the *Saengerfests* it is a pleasure to see each club's flag paraded in the march. The flag holds a bounty of ribbons flowing from the staff, each one a reminder of the choir's presence at

OLD PHOTO OF LUCKENBACH BAR

the festival. After World War II, carrying flags in Germany was prohibited. It was considered inappropriate because it reminded the citizens of Hitler's regime. However, here in Texas, the flag carrying has always continued unabated.

Mr. Mark Hierholzer, the club director since 1986, continues to preside over the society today. He directs two festivals a year, Mayfest and *Oktoberfest*. The youngest member of the club is fifty. There are no new younger members joining them. A grand tradition, spanning two continents—let's hope it isn't drawing to a close.

The Dast Ist Alles Fest (That's All)

At Luckenbach, the *Dast Ist Alles* Fest always takes place on Labor Day, signaling the end of summer. The celebration plays host to hundreds of local musicians. In 1995, it was held at the Grapetown dancehall and here was the blurb for the event, listing the eclectic musicians of the area. The names of the bands and musicians are especially interesting.

Grapetown Texas
Sunday September 3, 1995

Once again, the shady oaks and cool breezes around Grapetown Dance Hall beckon everyone to come spend an afternoon enjoying the friendship and family feeling of Das Ist Alles Fest. Come sit back and listen to the music of some of the Hill Country's finest musicians or just come out and relax in the laid-back atmosphere of Grapetown Hall. Food and drink will be available so please leave ice chests and pets at home. The gates open at 11:00 a.m. with music beginning at noon and lasting until 11:00 p.m. Entertainers this year include David Neal and Karen Zimmerman, Tim Schultz, Lee McCullough, Polkamatics, Gregg Cheser & the Pronto Brothers, Kent & Jenny Finlay, Lillian Stanfield & Loose Reed, Jimmy Lee Jones & the Texas Hill Country Band, Luckenbach Songbird Maggie Montgomery, Monte Montgomery, Geronimo Trevino, Too Strange for Sisterdale, and the Ben Beckendorf Band. So, come out and hear some of the finest music around!

MARY LEE EDWARDS

SHERIFF MARGE MUELLER

ROBBYN DODD

WHERE MARGE RULES

WILL the CIRCLE be UNBROKEN

Remembering Sheriff Marge and Ethel the Guinea Hen, and the Healing Power of Music

The smaller a place is, the more the big things in it are missed. I was mad when the souvenir hunters stole the old signs and antique firetruck. I smarted when the blacksmith shop and cotton gin washed away down Grape Creek in the 2002 flood. Even the voices of Hondo, Tex Schoffield "The Mouth" chili emcee, and Jalapeño Sam who ran armadillo races have faded into the moonlight. But the loudest scream ever heard will be the silence of the unique voice that accompanied the unique presence of our dear "Sheriff" Marge Mueller, who died July 25, 2002. She was 69.

Luckenbach's bartender, Sheriff Marge was truly Luckenbach's first citizen. Her family's presence in Luckenbach began in 1886. Her great-great-grandfather, August Engel, ran the post office in the rock house of Elizabeth and Benno Engel. Marge's great-great-uncle Adolf Engel was the first bartender. In 1970, when her great-uncle Benno Engel had emphysema, he put an ad in the paper that read simply, "Town for Sale," signaling the end of the 84-year long Engel ownership of Luckenbach.

Marge's parents lived on land in the Luckenbach community where they raised 60,000 chickens. Back in one of their pastures stands Luckenbach's original rock school building where airship inventor Jacob Brodbeck taught class.

Marge went to the newer, one-room brick Luckenbach School up the road by the Full Moon Inn. She wore overalls to school and had to sneak out to the barn with the other kids to speak the German language, which was prohibited during the '40s due to the war. Marge was elected Valedictorian and read poetry and speeches at the school closings in Engel Halle (later re-christened the Luckenbach dancehall). Even though the school closed down in the '60s, they continued to have commencement programs at the dancehall.

In 1970, after Hondo and Guich bought Luckenbach from Marge's Uncle Benno, they got to know the regular customers who'd been coming there for years. Oliver Ottmers (Marge's first husband) was one of the regulars who sat around there a lot. Marge would come down to get Oliver. Marge used to come to Luckenbach all dolled up in a dress and wearing hose, but she had to sit outside because at that time women weren't allowed in the bar. Hard to imagine.

Hondo, who gave titles to everyone said, "Marge, I'd like you to be my Sheriff." Hondo was self-proclaimed Mayor, Guich was Minister of Foreign Affairs and Roy Petsch was named Minister of Agriculture since he took the town's eggs to Austin to sell.

Next thing you know, Marge was manning the bar. For the next 33 years, Marge truly made everyone feel like they were indeed "Somebody in Luckenbach." The town motto may be "Everybody's Somebody in Luckenbach," but the second motto is "Don't Mess with Sheriff Marge!"

Marge's days of waiting demurely outside the bar dressed like a secretary were over. As the head bartender and "Sheriff", she soon came into her own. One time she reprimanded an unruly customer, "We don't need that kind of language here! Get on outta here!" The guy actually left.

Marge was never seen without her long braids and long rattlesnake earrings. Even her second husband, James Mueller, grew a long braid to match hers. She often wore short shorts with panty hose during the Seventies. But more visible than her image was her voice. Her voice carried plenty of authority. The way her voice projected, she could've been an actress in the pre-electronic days.

Guich remembered Marge came to work one day saying, "Oh, I'm so embarrassed. I was calling those damn kids to come home and all the neighbors' cows came up!" When I was talking to 90-year-old Mrs. Engel, who lived in the only house in Luckenbach, she asked if Marge was still working at Luckenbach, because she couldn't hear her yelling anymore, two blocks away.

Marge's husband James Mueller, "Deputy James," worked on the roads, grounds and dancehall at Luckenbach. Just having James around created more bar stories when news was slow. Like the time Marge hired the weekend washtub bass player Joe McCarthy, a carpenter by day, to build closets and cabinets at her house. Joe was overheard at the bar that next week saying Marge was getting a whole bunch of new drawers. James said, "Marge needs new drawers. Her old ones are all blowed out." The word spread fast all over town that Marge was getting new drawers.

Only a fool would underestimate Marge as a simple country girl bartender with a loud mouth. She was a true Texas woman: smart, strong and remarkable, with that classic German work ethic, but who also had a soft side and a loyal spirit. Her mind could quickly calculate how much ice and how many cases of beer we'd need for 1,000 people. On our first World's Fair in '76 she worked her fingers to frostbite conditions for 22 hours serving beer out of ice tubs, returning after only two hours sleep to pick up acres of

BIKERS COME TO LUCKENBACH

beer cans, "So the Sunday gospel singers wouldn't have to step on them," she said.

When wine was added to the bar menu, Marge had trouble using the corkscrew. She ingeniously invented her own Luckenbach corkscrew: a screw glued to a Phillips screwdriver, twisted with a pair of pliers.

For the young first-time visitor to Luckenbach, getting yelled at by Marge, for sins ranging from bringing your own beer to using rough language, was a rite of passage. Marge was such a good Sheriff because she had eyes in the back of her head.

When Austin had a bike rally that drew 30,000 motorcycles, Marge braced herself for at least half of them coming to Luckenbach. She had her hands full serving beer to the long lines of bikers. One burly guy who had been sitting at the bar was messing with Marge in a flirtatious way and said, "We need to get Marge a thong!" Marge quickly and loudly snapped back, "I wear my thongs on my feet!" The biker backed away slowly, having learned that you don't mess with Marge when she's busy.

Marge was also upset when one of the bikers burned rubber on the pavement in the shape of a peace sign when he left on his motorcycle. "I can hardly write him a citation for leaving a peace sign," laughed Marge.

Reporting crime and keeping the law in this peaceful place took some detective work. Marge thought someone went too far when they stole the handles off the two faucets in the ladies' restroom. "They didn't even have 'Luckenbach' written on them anywhere! Why would someone steal faucet handles for souvenirs?!" Marge said. The only clue she had figured out is that the thief was probably a female since the crime took place in the ladies' restroom.

The most tragic crime in Luckenbach was when Ethel, the six-year-old Guinea hen, was killed by a dog whose owner disregarded the leash law. Ethel had managed to outrun countless kids, dogs, critters, tourists and 15,000 of Willie's fans over the years. She had become the *Luckenbach Moon* newspaper's symbol and one of Marge's bar pets.

From time to time Luckenbach had a flock of Guinea fowl on the grounds. The Guinea fowl is popular on farms throughout Texas because they make such good watch dogs; especially for snakes. Anything strange that comes along sets the "Gennies" into their warning chant which can go on as long as they are disturbed. The Gennies were not real popular with the campers, as they would often wake up just at daylight and begin a ruckus that woke up the rooster, who began to crow. Sleeping any longer after all that avian racket commenced was out of the question.

Ethel was the only fowl in Luckenbach history who ever had her own bar tab. The bartenders would put it on Ethel's tab if someone wanted to buy her a package of peanuts. Ethel was such a show-off. And she helped the locals show off too. If Ethel knew you, you could hold a peanut up over her head between your thumb and forefinger, just like you'd do a dog, and she'd jump up and take it out of your fingers.

Who could forget the time Ethel stowed away in the Coors Light beer truck? What a surprise to Bubba the beer man when he opened the truck door and discovered her happily setting on a stack of beer boxes miles from Luckenbach. He immediately called Marge and reported that he had Ethel and would keep her safe in the warehouse until the next week when he delivered beer.

Marge had the idea to stuff (some say "mount") Ethel after her demise, and perch her as a permanent monument over the bar by Hondo's eagle. "I'll call the same guy who stuffed my snake!" she announced. Maggie Montgomery, aka "Magnolia Thunder Blossom," described Ethel's memorial: "Ethel was finally properly placed on her final perch in the beer joint during the St. Patrick's Day Mud Dauber Festival.

"Despite the cold weather the crowds numbered in the three digits instead of the two digits, which we sometimes draw for an occasion of this magnitude. A small group of reverent revelers assembled in the beer joint for a short commemorative ceremony for Ethel. Big Daddy Dauber raised all four of his arms and called for quiet. Mare VelAnne was present and gave a short eggstraordinary eulogy. I, Magnolia Thunder Blossom, recalled some eggsamples of Ethel's eggscapades and the ceremony ended with these and other Luckenbach Locals doing the "chicken dance" around the wood stove. Some said we were 'hot to trot'."

It's hard to imagine that during the 2002 Flood there was mud and water up over the bar. Marge admitted to laundering the money from the safe and cash registers. She took it home and dried it in her new dryer.

Marge became a cult figure because of her popularity. Her face was printed on T-shirts and koozies. People came to the bar to see her, hear her rough German accent, listen to details of history, and hear her speak German to the German visitors. She was a genuine, authentic piece of Texana who became endeared to everyone. Above all, Marge was our Ambassadress to the world. Proving that you never have to leave Luckenbach to be an effective peacemaker, she said, "Working at Luckenbach is like taking a trip around the world without the hassles of traveling. I have bonded with the world. It's a total communication system without leaving home. Isn't that wonderful?" Lastly, Marge added, "Luckenbach is a place where you can come and be yourself. It's a place where people come together. We need one in every state!"

As someone who was born, raised, educated in, worked at, and never left Luckenbach, her legend was home-grown. Laughingly, I told Guich Koock, "I guess Marge graduated from school and never has left Luckenbach." His answer, "Well, who'd ever want to leave?!"

The Luckenbach bar was home to Marge, and to home she was returned. A wake was held for her in the dance hall. A memorial service, presided over by Episcopal priest, the Rev. Jane Patterson, formed a somber procession to the Hal John Wimberly Memorial Campfire site across Grape Creek. Some of her ashes were mingled with the ashes of others who'd chosen that locale for their monument.

The place where she'd worked for 33 years, a 2' x 12' area behind the bar, was also a holy place. So, it was fitting that the rest of her ashes be ensconced in the blue enamel coffee pot (which also functioned as her tip jar) up in the corner of the bar ceiling next to a cobwebbed traffic light, only inches away from the permanent final perch of the dear taxidermed body of Ethel the Guinea hen. In such and exalted and elevated locale, her spirit could still hover over the thousands to whom she'd served a beer, a smile, and a hello.

The mystique of Luckenbach is the sum of legendary people whose uniqueness has shaped and colored its history. However fragile the physical place, the spirit of these people will never die here. Gary P. Nunn first met Marge in 1973 during the recording of Jerry Jeff Walker's landmark album, *¡Viva Terlingua!* "She's always been the most colorful character with an unstoppable personality," he said. "There won't be any replacing her. Like Hondo, she'll be gone, but never be forgotten."

Although Marge's voice is silent now, it's been memorialized in Luckenbach's "Twelve Days of Christmas" song, written by another co-bartender, Jimmy Lee Jones, with the help of Luckenbach Songbird Maggie Montgomery.

TWELVE DAYS OF CHRISTMAS IN LUCKENBACH

(sung to the traditional tune)
On the 12th day of Christmas
In Luckenbach you'll see
12 bowls of chili
11 couples dancin'
10 tattooed bikers
9 readers MOONin'
8 feral bachelors
7 Ladies Lynchin'
A 6-pack for me
M-A-R-G-E Y-E-L-L-S AT J-A-M-E-S
4 locals drinkin'
3 pickers pickin'
2 dogs in heat
And Ethel in an oak treeeeeee!

We Were Counted

Me and Mama spent Wednesday of this week at Luckenbach standin' by the flagpole wavin' at airplanes. You know, not many folks do that anymore... If one of them planes waves back it makes you feel strong and tall, like when me and Mama go riding down the highway and run over that little rubber hose that counts cars and goes blump-blump. Boy, it makes us sit tall and look around and see if anybody is watching, because we very seldom ever get counted in Luckenbach.

– Hondo, alias Peter Cedarstacker

Hondo gave us a stage for amateur musicians, the pickers circle. I thought we should have one big pickers circle,

– Abbey Road.

As long as there's the big live oaks to gather under and the Luckenbach stove to sit around, there will be music. Music: an escape, a connection, happiness, healing, heaven; the power to transform, to remove barriers and walls. Long live the pickers' circles.

One of the grandest most emotional moments I ever experienced at Luckenbach was on August 23, 2009, when those at Luckenbach were counted for a fundraiser called "Pickin' for the Record." A *Guinness Book of World Record* placeholder was broken for the most guitar players gathered at one time to play continuously for at least five minutes. The previous record, held in Germany, was broken with an unofficial (so far) count of 1859. The day before our event, Elvis Presley's guitar player held a similar event in Arkansas and only signed up 800 pickers.

But at Luckenbach, we knocked it out of the park. Barbara Mann said, "I was stuck in the ticket booth all day. The line never ended. They just kept comin' at me from the parking lot until 1918 signed up."

The brainstormers behind the record-breaking event were Abbey Road, Luckenbach events coordinator; Dallas Allen, director of the Kerrville Folk Festival; Craig Hillis, who is a western writer, a veteran musician, and an ex-Gonzo band member; and Charlie Gallagher, veteran and promoter of Voices of a Grateful Nation, a group which uses music as a medium to support military veterans. The purpose was to raise funds for the Welcome Home Project's veterans' endowment for traumatic brain injuries. The idea was to perpetuate the tradition of Texas music at its official shrine, namely Luckenbach; to provide a place for pro and amateur alike who all share the story, joy and love that music produces.

Maggie Montgomery, Luckenbach Songbird and mother of blues guitar virtuoso Monte Montgomery (who grew up at Luckenbach

1,918 PICKERS PLAYING "LET'S GO TO LUCKENBACH TEXAS"

FUNDRAISER FOR
VOICES OF A GRATEFUL NATION'S
VETERANS WITH BRAIN INJURIES

since he was ten years old), got her son back home and involved. Gibson Guitars was part of it. In honor of Les Paul's recent death (at 94) Gibson donated a Les Paul guitar to be raffled off at the event. Monte was asked to play a tribute on it to Les Paul, in the form of "The Star-Spangled Banner" and "Little Wings." Boy, you should have been there to hear that!

Musicians Bo Porter, Matt Powell, Buddy Lee (himself a wounded vet), Doug Moreland, Roger Creager, Jeff Plankenhorn, Gary P. Nunn, Jaime Oldaker, and John Inmon were there for the on-stage warm up. Group Song Leaders were Dow Patterson and Roger Creager, with Monte accompanying the group on his free-form blues-style guitar.

The tune up of 2000 guitars strumming sounded like a giant swarm of buzzing bees. To ask anyone before the actual playing in unison of the famous familiar song "Let's Go to Luckenbach, Texas," one would just say, "It's another party at Luckenbach. We want to participate. We want to support the wounded warriors."

But *after* the real experience comments would change to more emotional feelings. "Awesome. Wonderful. Everybody *is* somebody here. Harmony. Love."

I was thinking, "unity." Unifying 2000 music-makers for five minutes. Families can't even do that. It was powerful. I cried. My son, Sky Patterson (Hondo's grandson) commented, "Hondo liked to count people at Luckenbach by throwing a garden hose across the road, like it was a real traffic counter. Today we were counted! My reaction while I was playing my guitar? I laughed." A big crowd in 100° heat? It didn't bother anyone. The cause was big. The mood was calm and peaceful. People wanted to be there. If you weren't, you missed a unique, great experience. Almost 3500 people came through those gates that day.

The Original Magic of Luckenbach Texas (The First of the Pickers' Circles)

Of all the Saturday nights spent at Luckenbach, the one I will always remember most fondly occurred in one evening in1973. We were all sitting under the trees with the chickens, along with Ruff, the alcoholic rooster, and a sprinkling of lightning bugs.

The nighttime chill moved our small, friendly group into the tiny bar to huddle around the potbelly stove. Ruff followed, hoping for more of the beer that Hondo would pour into a bottle cap. Sheriff Marge chased Oink Van Gogh, the one-eared pig, out of the bar. The door burst open. A few more old friends carried in a violin, guitar and a Jamaican bass. Someone produced a harmonica. Another drug up a washtub bass. Porfie Cantu had his accordion. A round of beers went forth. We all lifted our beers in a toast toward the ceiling, to the empty chair Hondo'd put in the cobwebbed corner in memory of Benny Luckenbach, who would come with his Chihuahua every day to start his cocktail hour as early as three p.m.

The chair held a sign, "Reserved for Benny." He'd sit there like a permanent fixture, petting his Chihuahua and raising our hair with his strong language. One night he couldn't get his truck started, so he slept in the loft over the bar. He told Hondo when he woke up he thought he'd died and gone to heaven, waking up in a beer joint. A small sign in Hondo's handwriting behind the bar read, "If you're drinking to forget, pay in advance." The music began to flow.

Guich Koock performed an accurate rendition of a Southern Baptist black clergyman preaching a sermon. Then he sang an old slave song, shifting into "High Noon," Tex Ritter-style, then ending in "Jalisco," which Hondo punctuated with Mexican *gritos*. At its conclusion, Hondo played "When the Saints Go Marching In" on a kazoo hidden in an old plumbing p-trap, sliding the joint like a trombone.

"Accompany me on the guitarlet, Guich!" The guitarlet was, naturally, a toilet seat strung with guitar strings. "We're the Luckenbach Comodians!"

The hysteria subsided. The single kerosene lamp glowed softly. C.C. Gibbons, a prominent member of the Houston Symphony, sobered everyone up merely by unlatching her violin case. Not long after, she began to draw her bow slowly across the strings, and our ears recognized the foot-stompin' "Cotton-Eyed Joe." The outsider was immediately respected.

Porfie Cantu played a German favorite, the "Beer Barrel Polka" on his accordion. When he played "Jesusita en Chihuahua," Hondo danced the polka around the stove. The guitar, ceremoniously passed around the circle, came to my husband Dow and me.

Hondo immediately put us on a pedestal by shushing everyone as we sang his favorite, "Rivers of Texas." When it was Hondo's turn, his weathered face and twinkling eyes became animated. He sang songs that painted pictures of canyons, sunsets, whispering sands, tumbleweeds. His voice rang with the sentiment he felt over the passing of a romantic era he once knew. He saved the best for last, "Que Puntada!," which he performed loudly snapping his guitar strings and slapping the guitar box in true *Huapango* style.

The times I cherished most with my father were those hours spent in his singing presence. I was spellbound. We lost ourselves, performer and listener, father and daughter, within that magical world that music brought home to our hearts.

After everyone had gone, Ruff was too drunk to fly up to his roost. So, Hondo gently lifted him to his oak tree perch. "Gollee! Look at that moon, Guich!" Hondo exclaimed. "Don't tell anyone we have such a *big* moon for such a *small* town!"

RUFF, THE ALCOHOLIC ROOSTER

LARRY UPSHAW, TEXAS HIGHWAYS

GUICH AND BENNY LUCKENBACH

RICHARD PRUITT

CHERISHED TIMES WITH HONDO

EPILOGUE

Hondo Crouch, *Reinventor*

In conclusion, the Trail of Fame at Luckenbach that began with the illustrious 19th century "Somebodies" leads straight to the 20th century and the one and only Hondo Crouch. Hondo earns his "Somebodies" membership by virtue of possessing some of the same attributes as those pioneers: They were all revolutionaries, with unstoppable imaginations. Their spirits were fiercely independent, free, tough and tenacious enough to conquer challenges and heartbreak. They were peacemakers, treating all with equality; trying to save the world with literature, music, humor, and laid-back fun. The Germans may have gotten to Luckenbach first. But Hondo, with a little help from Jerry Jeff and Waylon Jennings, reinvented it and branded it, and took it to the world. He made the little Hill Country ghost town a state of mind and a magnet for romantics everywhere.

In summary, Hondo, a "reinventor," reigned as "Clown Prince" over his little principality, Population 4, at the figurative height of the season. He was a philosopher, a Texas humorist, raconteur, writer, poet, music man, entertainer, rancher, and athlete. His calling card read "Imagineer, Authorized Distributor."

THE BAR DOOR IS ON DISPLAY IN THE COLLECTION "OUTLAWS AND ARMADILLOS, THE ROARING '70s" AT NASHVILLE'S COUNTRY MUSIC HALL OF FAME MUSEUM

He made himself mayor, quickly acquired one parking meter, and a mailbox perched on a tall pole for airmail. He held "suppo-siums," taught adults how to "p'like" (play-like) and laugh at themselves. He was a peacemaker, pulling together hippies, rednecks and those in between. His idea of war was not shooting bullets or cannon balls, but rather firing chicken feathers out of a homemade cannon, and passing out Purple Hearts to whoever fell down best.

Rev. David Redding, a writer from Ohio who visited Hondo, likened him to an Elizabethan court jester, the Fool, who was there not only to entertain but to be a guard of honor, putting down smugness, deflating the arrogant and lifting up the little guy. Redding said the clown in the king's court was an unpredictable scamp who mirrors our absurdity.

It wasn't all fun and games. Hondo means "deep" in Spanish. Hondo's humor hid his deep sadness and personal tragedies; namely, his father's suicide while Hondo was at UT, his exquisite son's mental illness and eventual suicide, his divorce, and the feeling that he "never made it," was never "successful." Hondo was like Pagliacci, the clown who cried on the inside but laughed on the outside. He embraced both sorrow and joy at once. Clowns, jesters, fools like Hondo are lonely, set apart, earthy, untamable. But their childlike simplicity and seeming innocence are appealing to common folk and envied by intellectuals. He was the supremely wise Fool.

The secret to a truly successful clown is to get the audience to love him and to love itself. He has been branded a Texas folk hero, meaning he is loved by the people forever. As Charles John Quarto's poem says, "Hondo, he drew a lasso 'round our hearts/And drew us to his side/He gave wisdom out like Halloween candy."

As a young college student, he fashioned himself after the great "Mr. Texas," author and folklorist J. Frank Dobie, his teacher at the University of Texas in the '30s, whom he affectionately called

"Uncle Frank." As Dobie's student in his first and most famous class, "Guide to Life and Literature of the Southwest," Hondo was influenced to keep Texas folklore alive by the deeply regional way he lived, dressed, wrote, and told stories. He became Texas folklore. Outsiders think Texas is about bigness and braggarts. Hondo emphasized the small and intimate.

Hondo wouldn't ever believe it, but he could fairly be called an entrepreneur. An entrepreneur is someone who has a dream and is consistently faithful to it and doesn't let anything deter him from it; like when Hondo said at 18, "I'm different. I'm going to be important someday." His creativity, writings and humor focused on being kind of a service, rather than an idea for making money, which he never did. His riches were those of the spirit. The life of Hondo Crouch made Texas a better place.

Once I knew this little man
He was only ten feet tall
He had a sparkle in his eye
Although he was a little off the wall
He had some yarns to tell you
And you knew every word was true
From the happy little man in the cowboy hat
With tobacco stains on his boots

Chorus:
Livin' and lovin' Hondo
He was kickin' up his heels wherever he'd go
Livin' and lovin' Hondo
He was a one-man rodeo
Livin' and lovin' Hondo
He was puttin' on a show wherever he'd go
Livin' and lovin' Hondo
He was dancin' with a dosey-do

When the good Lord made ol' Hondo
Well, he threw away the mold
He was the last of the oldtime buckaroos

With a heart of solid gold
He finally got so many friends
He had to buy himself a town
So he bought a place called Luckenbach
Ten a month and twenty down

Ain't nobody ever met a man
That didn't walk off with a smile
He had that special magic
I guess that you could call it style
He didn't care who came to pick
Or set upon his couch
'Cause everybody's somebody
In the heart of Hondo Crouch.

"Livin' and Lovin' Hondo"
Written in the parking lot moments
before Hondo's memorial service at
St Barnabas Episcopal Church,
– Rick Beresford

Ferdinand von Roemer, who was called the "Father of Texas Geology," and who bravely accompanied Baron Meusebach to offer peace to the Comanches, once stood on a hill among scattered buffalo skulls, overlooking Fredericksburg in 1847. There he observed the fledgling town of 600 inhabitants with their quickly-made log houses with roofs of dried mud, grass or canvas. An early eyewitness to the immigrant struggles, he wrote about the farming communities of Luckenbach, Sisterdale and Grapetown in his book *Roemer's Texas.*

I live and stand here now, among these same hills, observing from afar passersby who are stopping on the highway to photograph and admire a sea of solid springtime bluebonnets. There's a constant roar and vibration of traffic and motorcycles, serpentining their way between Luckenbach and Sisterdale. Gated developments dot the once extensively-forested area. The tree stumps in the 1847

Main Street of Fredericksburg have been replaced by pedestrians carrying shopping bags, tourists fighting over parking places, banners stretched across the street advertising festivals. Our popular Hill Country has become the hub of Spring Breakers, foreign traffic, tourists of all descriptions. Like Luckenbach, it risks being loved to death.

Still, I cherish this land and the people who helped settle it. The Hill Country gives us water, food, wine, recreation, beauty, views and open spaces. Let's not forget how to find the North Star, to know the difference between a pin tail and a cotton tail (duck and rabbit, respectively). I leave you with the 1847 quote from Roemer upon his departure from Texas to return to Germany—just to remember how it once was. Yes, visiting here leaves people, even hard-headed old German botanists, with warm memories.

> *I had developed interest and love for the beautiful land of meadows which faces a bright future: and it filled my heart with sadness to be compelled to bid it farewell forever. However there remains with me agreeable and rich memories and I will always follow from the distance the further development of this country with great interest. May its wide green prairies become the home of a large and happy population.*

LIVIN' AND LOVIN' HONDO

LUCKENBACH ARCHIVES

LUCKENBACH PARKING LOT

DAYNA DEHOYOS

ABOUT THE AUTHOR

Becky is the author of two memoirs of the two legends in her life. The Texana bestseller, *Hondo, My Father,* (1979) (endorsed by James A. Michener) is about her hilarious but poignant life with Hondo, the self-proclaimed Mayor of Luckenbach. She was co-owner of Luckenbach for twenty-four years, during which she wrote a column, "Everybody's Somebody" for the *Luckenbach Moon.* Her most recent book, *The Ranch That Was Us,* (2012) (with a foreword by Willie Nelson), is an epic saga of her grandfather, Adolf Stieler, the "Angora Goat King of the World" in the '40s. Illustrated with fifty of her paintings, it was required reading for the James Michener School of Creative Writing at the University of Texas.

She is a painter, liturgical artist, sewn appliqued tapestries for many churches and individuals, created Hondo's Hats line and designed western clothing.

A fifth generation Texan, Becky was raised on her parents' ranch not far from Luckenbach. She lives on the 130-year-old Stieler Home Ranch headquarters in Comfort, Texas.

> *"As a writer, Becky is a chip off one of her father Hondo's whittlings. She has his same eagle-eye observations, as well as a poetic voice of truth and clarity."*
>
> – Willie Nelson

BIBLIOGRAPHY

Books

Burrier, Sr. William Paul

Biographies of Individuals Involved in the Nueces River Battle/ Massacre. Self-published, Leakey, Texas. 2004–2006

Gillespie County Historical Society

Pioneers in God's Hills, Vol. 1, Von Beckmann-Jones, Austin, Texas. 1960.

Gilliam, Luke and Guy Rogers III

Pat Green's Dance Halls and Dreamers, Dreamers Publishing, LLC., University of Texas Press, 2008.

Heck, Bryan & Hilliard, Howard

Luckenbach, Texas Celebrated, 1974.

King, Irene Marschall

John O. Meusebach, University of Texas Press, 1967.

Patterson, Becky Crouch

Hondo, My Father, Shoal Creek Pub. 1979.

Patterson, Becky Crouch

The Ranch That Was Us, Trinity University Press, 2012.

Porter, Jenny Lind

El Sol Colorado, Southwestern Classics Press, Austin, TX, 2001.

Ransleben, Guido E.

A Hundred Years of Comfort in Texas: A Centennial History , San Antonio, 1954.

Roemer, Ferdinand Von

Roemer's Texas, Bonn, Germany, 1849.

Tatsch, Anita

Jacob Brodbeck Reached for the Texas Skies, Dietel & Son Printing, Fredericksburg, TX, 1986.

Papers & Periodicals

Boening, Heinrich

"History of the Fredericksburg, Texas Hermannsohne Gemischter Chor," 2015.

Crouch, Hondo (alias Peter Cedarstacker)

"Cedar Creek Clippings", *The Comfort News*, (1969–1974).

Davis, John T.

"The Song" and McNeese, Don, "Back to the Basics in Luckenbach," *Austin American-Statesman*, June 30, 1996.

Fowler, Gene

"Musical Frontier," *Texas Co-op Power*, January 2018.

Goodspeed, John

"Back to the Basics," *San Antonio Express-News*, May 30, 2004.

Handbook of Texas online, Texas State Historical Association

Pinta Trail map

Luckenbach Monthly Moon

Luckenbach, Texas, Inc. John Raven, Becky Crouch Patterson, Maggie Montgomery, writers.

Makin, Annelise

"Surviving the Hangebund Times: The Murder of the German Unionists in Fredericksburg". *German Life*, December/January 2018. pp. 26–9.

Milner, Jay

"Outlaws Love Texas," *Texas Music*, May 1976.

Nelson, Willie

"Willie Nelson Remembers Hondo," *Luckenbach Monthly Moon*, January 21, 1978.

Robenalt, Jefery

"A Glimpse of Texas Past", August 1, 2017, texasescapes.com

Spong, John

"That Seventies Show," *Texas Monthly*, April 2012.

Stowers, Carlton

"Hondo Crouch and His Backwoods Camelot," *Scene Magazine, Dallas Morning News*, May 1976.

Walker, Jerry Jeff,

"*¡Viva Terlingua!*" liner notes.

Wilkinson, David

"Important Texas Music:*¡Viva Terlingua!*" April 6, 2013.

Wright, Lawrence,

"The Future is Texas," *The New Yorker*, July 10 & 17, 2017.

Poems

"Luckenbach Moon"

Hondo Crouch, (1973) © Grape Creek Music.

"Luckenbach Daylight"

Hondo Crouch, (1979) © Grape Creek Music.

Quarto, Charles John

"His Heart Was So Full of Mischief", Poems from the poetry opera "South by Southwest" © Charles John Quarto, 1978.

Songs

"A Long Way to Go"

Davin Jones, Nunn Publishing Company, 1996.

"Everybody's Somebody in Luckenbach"

Ted & Birdie Holliday

"Hondo's Lament"

Naomi Shihab Nye & John Paul Walters, 1976.

"Let's Go to Luckenbach, Texas—Back to the Basics"

Bobby Emmons & Chip Momans, Universal Music Publishing Group, 1977.

"Livin' and Lovin' Hondo"

Rick Beresford, Universal Music Careers, BMI. 1977.

"London Homesick Blues"

Gary P. Nunn, Nunn Publishing Company. 1983.

"Lookin Back at Luckenbach"

Tommy Alverson & Noel Clement, Four-Four Music Sesac.

"Movin' On"

Jerry Jeff Walker, Groper Music, 1993.

"Road Trip"

Gary P. Nunn, Nunn Publishing Company, 1994.

"Terlingua Sky"

Billy Joe Shaver, Nunn Publishing Company, 1991.

"The Flyboy and the Kid"

Rodney Crowell, New West Records, Sony ATV Milene Music, ASCAP, 2014.

"The Randall Knife"

Guy Clark, EMI April Music, Inc., 1983.

"Twelve Days of Christmas at Luckenbach"

Jimmy Lee Jones & Maggie Montgomery, Luckenbach Monthly Moon, 1992.

"Truck Song"

Jerry Jeff Walker, Groper Music, 1989.

"Viva Luckenbach"

Jerry Jeff Walker, Groper Music, 1994.

IN APPRECIATION

To my parents Shatzie and Hondo Crouch, for their simple greatness, wit and lifestyle, raising us kids like a wild but cultured tribe of Indians; for their lifelong dedication to conservation, history, folklore, and relics; teaching us old is beautiful and nothing is ugly.

To Guich Koock, for his courageous insight and outrageous creativity.

To De Foster, his ambitious encouragement, otherwise this book would not exist. I was asked to write my two previous books. But De, calling me the "Evangelist of Luckenbach", commanded this one. Followed by Gary P. Nunn's "Get 'er done!"

To Caren Richardson, always my right and left hand, taking all my scrawled hand-written yellow pages and typing them into neat white ones, over and over.

To Bridgette Neidre, my German wordsmith, *danke.*

To my editor John T. Davis, perfect for this job, combing through every word, making it into a real book.

To John Phillip Santos, whose foreword is like a pedestal, a door for my book. I am privileged to have your brilliant words.

To Backstage Design Studios, endlessly inventive, clever Shauna and Sarah Dodds. They are Grammy Award winning and Grammy nominated designers for the Texas music industry and genius designers of this book's jacket cover.

And a special thanks to Terry Sherrell and George Anne Byfield, the entire staff of OneTouchPoint-Southwest Printing, for their patience, hard work and excellence.

Thank you, historians, for getting it all down in the nick of time and preserving it: Anita Tatsch, granddaughter of Jacob Brodbeck; Heinrich Boenig and Regina Rosenwinkle, Saengerfest singers; Anne Stewart, Comfort's emergency historian.

Thank you, makers and keepers of beauty: songwriters, poets, photographers. Especially, for the eyes and lenses of Robbyn Dodd, Luckenbach's official photographer, for her time, and for capturing the day and night life. Including, photographers from *Scene Magazine* of the *Dallas Morning News*, the *Fredericksburg Standard, Austin American-Statesman, Texas Highways and Public Transportation*, Tom Wilkes, Bryan Heck, Howard Hilliard, Monk Vance, De Foster, Dayna DeHoyos, Kathryn Millan, Larry Upshaw, Mike Marvins, Jim McGuire, Brian Kanof, Scott Newman, Ruth and Gary P. Nunn, Pat O'Bryan, Richard Pruitt, Andy Reisburg, Mary Lee Edwards, Ed Purvis, Chris Regas, Reed Harp, Nancy Goldfarb, Gerald Crawford, Ron Jones, the artwork of Jim Franklin, and Donna Lilly of Busy Bee Graphics,

Thank you, Dow Patterson, for your help.

Thank you, John Raven (aka Bad McFad) for being there.

Thank you to the entire staff of Luckenbach: Managers of Operations, Store, Bar, Grounds, Event Planners, and some forty-five helpers, security, road dogs, picker circle leaders; in great appreciation to Maggie Montgomery and Janie Schofield, who've been here since the beginning, faithful and eternal Presidents of the Luckenbach Ladies Lynching League. Onward, guardians of Hondo's dream, Cris Crouch Graham and Kit Patterson. Your hard work, whether it's for three or three thousand, keeps Luckenbach the center of the universe.

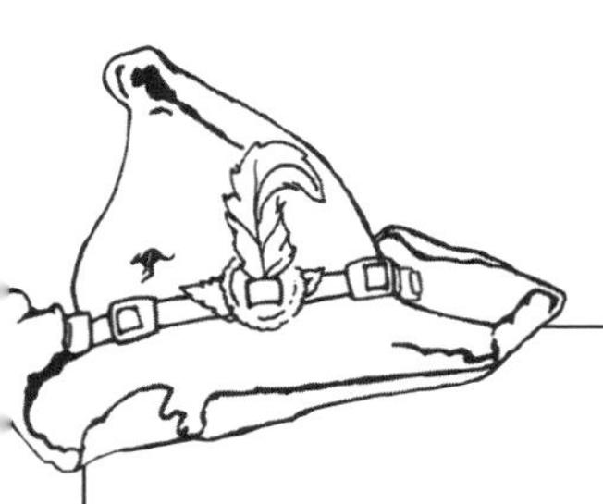

ROBBYN DODD

KIT PATTERSON, CEO, PREZ

ROBBYN DODD

“THANK YOU LUCKENBACH DANCEHALL!” - RIVER BOT[illegible]M BO[illegible]

YOU CAN *tell a* BOOK *by its* COVER

What's on the cover is as important as what's inside. This jacket cover is designed by multi-Grammy Award winning Backstage Design Studio sisters Shauna and Sarah Dodds, two of the most creative five-star designers for packaging Texas music, albums, and books. The cover, loaded with hidden layers of rich meaning and magical images, shows four facets of Luckenbach in the corners. A galaxy of **stars** from the universe is scattered over a huge **moon** behind the store. (*People won't believe we have such a big moon for such a small town.*—Hondo)

INVENTORS: Framed by an **engineer's compass**, is the 1861 "**airship**" invented by Luckenbach's Jacob Brodbeck.

PEACEMAKERS: Framed by peace symbols, a **broken arrow and white feather**, for the 1847 Peace Treaty between the Comanches and the Hill Country German immigrants. **Buffalo skulls**, later found scattered over the hills, were used by the Comanches for headdresses. **Pansies** are a long-established symbol of the **German Free-thinkers**. Panseé—French for "thought", the flower resembles a human face, an intellectual.

MUSIC MAKERS: Luckenbach, past and present, has always been a shrine for Texas music. It was a center for Saengerfests of the 1850s, and now of pickers circles for both amateur and professionals.

The **armadillo**, symbol for 1970s Outlaw Music which found its roots there, united the redneck with the hippie. The **Guinea hen**, a Luckenbach store icon.

IMAGINEERS: The magician Hondo, with his **2-knot rope trick**, and his stories of the wasp **mud dauber**, the "national bird of Luckenbach". **Grapes** are for Luckenbach's original name, **Grape Creek**, and the prophetic prediction from Fredericksburg founder Meusebach in 1847, that soil conditions here were perfect for grapes, vineyards, wine making.

SPINE: **Propeller plane** dragging banner reminds us of the dog-fight stories of airplanes in Luckenbach skies.

BACK COVER: **Globe with string around it and finger** alludes to both the story showing **proof** that Luckenbach really is in the center of the universe, and **Hondo's finger pointing** on the "*Viva Terlingua*" album cover art. Also, **Hondo's signature hat, Lone Star Longneck Beer**, an icon for 70s Outlaw music, and Ruff, the alcoholic **rooster**.

THANK YOU, Sarah and Shauna, for such depth of thought, heart and soul, research, detail, with which you gift-wrapped my book.

—Becky Patterson

Luckenbach Team –

Thank you
for a *gemütlich** evening!
It was wonderful
to have such a gathering
of folks to share the
old time camaraderie for
which Luckenbach was known!
I especially appreciate
all your efforts and
work – and I am proud
of your results –

Shatzie Crouch

Sept 30, 2008

*cheerful, pleasant, commonly associated with the tenor of a German beer garden